Activities for
Any Novel

By Nancy Polette

Pieces of Learning

© 1999 Nancy Polette
1999 First Published
by Pieces of Learning

www.piecesoflearning.com
CLC0223
ISBN 1-880505-39-8

Printed in the U.S.A.

Many of the images used herein were obtained from IMSI's Master Clip/Master Photos© Collection, 1895 Francisco Blvd. East, San Rafael, CA 94901-5506, USA
For a complete catalog of products contact Pieces of Learning or
visit our Website at www.piecesoflearning.com

Table of Contents

Strategies for Integration Which Incorporate the Six Keys to Learning

Pre Reading Strategies

Post Reading Strategies

INTRODUCTION

SIX KEYS TO LEARNING

How do people learn best? There are literally hundreds of research studies that identify six factors that are essential to successful learning regardless of the age of the learner.

Learning is **SOCIAL**. We learn best with and from other people. No one learns to speak in an isolated environment. Yet much of what takes place in an educational setting is isolated skill and drill.

Learning begins with the learner's **EXPERIENCE**. All that we have learned is based on previous knowledge. We make sense of new information by searching the brain's storehouse for appropriate referents. The sentence, *"The notes were sour because the seams split,"* makes little sense to most people. Yet, if you were an experienced bagpipe player it would make perfect sense based on your experience with bagpipes.

Successful learning requires **RISK TAKING**. If we know the answers, we don't have to think. If we know the answers there is no point in reading the material that contains the answers. By RISK TAKING we mean that guessing is encouraged.

Give students a short true/false test about the material they are to read BEFORE reading. Encourage guessing. Then ask students to read the material to support or deny their guesses. Students who are focused this way on a topic are far more likely to understand and retain the material. True learning stresses **MEANING**. Traditional classrooms have long focused on the *"what did it say?"* kinds of questions by asking who was in the story or where did Columbus land first in the New World? Questions better asked would be:

"Which character underwent the greatest change in the story and why do you think this is true?"
Or
"What would be the effects on Spain of the discoveries of Columbus?"

Learning must be **ACTIVE**. No one learns by sitting and listening. Students must be given many ways to process information and a variety of ways in which to encode it. Students need to be encouraged to show their understanding of a topic by organizing the information in a new way. This is the mark of a truly literate person.

Effective learning mandates **CHOICE**. The choice could be as simple as choosing two of ten questions to answer at the end of a social studies chapter or as challenging as determining the best product to use in sharing information on a topic.

Consider a typical assignment: *"Read chapter X and answer the questions at the end of the chapter."* There is nothing **SOCIAL** about this. We do not know if the learner has any **EXPERIENCE** with the topic or not. There is no **RISK TAKING** involved. It is hard to say what **MEANING,** if any, the student will get from the material.

Some students may **ACTIVELY** read the material while many will not. There is no **CHOICE**. Everyone is expected to read the same material and answer the same questions. This typical assignment is totally incompatible with how people learn.

The strategies in this book incorporate the **SIX KEYS TO LEARNING** and are designed for easy integration within and among the disciplines. While the examples given are generally from the classics of children's literature, these strategies can be used with ANY novel.

WHAT RESEARCH SAYS

The strategies presented in this book are supported by the research.

"Children who are read to from quality children's literature score higher on tests of vocabulary and reading comprehension than children who are not read to."

Chomsky, Carol. "Stages in Language Development from Reading Exposure." *HARVARD EDUCATIONAL REVIEW* Feb. 1972.

"Reading to children not only stimulates thought and brings forms of literature to children they might not ordinarily read...but...it also helps improve writing styles through hearing the vocabulary, sentence construction, grammar and syntactic arrangements, organization and approach used by other writers."

Blake, Howard E. "Written Composition in English Primary Schools." *Elementary English* Oct. 1971: 605-616.

"Twenty-one books were used as read-alouds with one group of students and as storytelling vehicles with an experimental group. Those in the experimental (storytelling) group made the largest gains in use of words and increased length in their own speech and in increased vocabulary knowledge on tests of basic skills."

Isbell, R.G.T. "A Study of the Effects of Two Modes of Presenting Literature." University of Tennessee. 1979.

"Recent research has suggested that background knowledge is a major, if not the major, determinant of text comprehension."

Pearson, P. David. "Asking Questions About Stories." *Genn Occasional Paper Number 15* 1982.

"Of 132 fifth grade students taught poetry combined with music, 87% wanted to study poems with music the next year and 85% thought that studying poetry with music helped them to learn new things."

Demetrales, P. Lehigh University, 1986.

"Research shows that neurological impressioning is a proven method for helping children acquire the patterns of language."

Healy, Dr. Jane. Your Child's Growing Mind. Doubleday, 1987.

"Children should develop skills in the context in which they will ultimately be used. This approach used with disabled 5th graders showed average gains of more than one year after only seven months of instruction."

Larrick, Nancy. "Illiteracy Starts Too Soon." *Phi Delta Kappan* Nov. 1987.

"Children need to rehearse before they write. A change or elaboration in rehearsal such as planning a story may lead to a more sophisticated piece. Children will grow as writers in classrooms where active rehearsal is encouraged."

Graves, Donald. *Language Arts* Oct. 1979.

"Placement of questions affect what is retained by the reader. If students are to interrelate information then pre-questions that require an interpretative level of response are essential."

Vacca, R.T. *Content Area Reading*. Little-Brown, 1981.

SELECTED OBJECTIVES

READING/LANGUAGE ARTS

The student will:

R1. Use appropriate letter-sound, structural and contextual strategies in identifying unknown words.

R2. Demonstrate an understanding of expository and narrative text by retelling, answering or formulating questions.

R3. Make judgments, infer an author's attitude, predict outcomes, draw conclusions based on evidence from the text.

R4. Recognize persuasive language, stereotypes, fallacy in argument and statements of bias based on evidence in the text.

R5. Use inductive reasoning to form generalizations.

R6. Use the conventions of written language correctly including spelling, capitalization, sentence structure, paragraph development, punctuation and correct use of parts of speech in producing clear writing.

R7. Listen attentively and critically.

R8. Develop oral language facility using the conventions of speech.

R9. Demonstrate an understanding of text by organizing main ideas and supporting details to encode information in a variety of ways.

CLC0223 Pieces of Learning

SOCIAL STUDIES/SCIENCE

The student will:

S1. Acquire, analyze, interpret and communicate information or data by observing, estimating, measuring and recognizing changes over time.

S2. Sequence, order and classify information.

S3. Form definitions based on observations and infer, generalize and predict outcomes.

S4. Identify a problem, formulate and evaluate alternative solutions.

S5. Draw conclusions about processes or outcomes and relate or apply knowledge gained.

S6. Form a hypothesis and design or construct a scientific investigation.

S7. Interpret information related to historical or geographical concepts.

S8. Use problem-solving and decision-making skills as they apply to social studies data.

S9. Demonstrate an understanding of civic values, American and other economic and political systems and cultural factors that affect human behavior.

S10. Understand and use the following thinking processes: analyze, classify, compare, contrast, create, determine, distinguish, evaluate, identify, interpret, sequence and summarize.

A NOVEL GUIDE CHECKLIST

For any novel you can create your own novel guide activities. You may want to include the following contents

- ✓ Information about the book
- ✓ Information about the author
- ✓ Vocabulary words to group and/or use in sentences
- ✓ Open-ended sentence starters
- ✓ Higher order discussion questions
- ✓ Chapter summaries (2-3 sentences)
- ✓ Eight to ten literature related activities to allow for research . . .

  . . . to introduce reading, writing and thinking skills
  . . . to review skills
  . . . to allow for student response to character, setting, plot, mood, point-of-view or theme of the book

- ✓ Clear procedure for evaluating projects

Combine content, process, and product with different strategies.

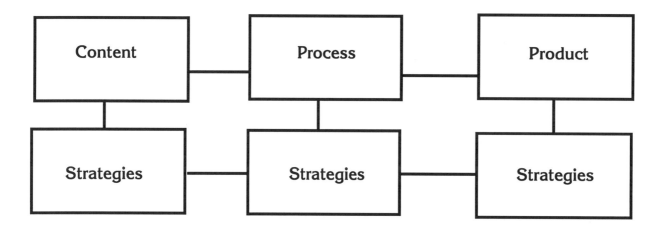

STRATEGIES FOR INTEGRATION
WHICH INCORPORATE
THE SIX KEYS TO LEARNING

PRE READING STRATEGIES

Strategy One: Categorizing New Vocabulary

Provide students with a list of vocabulary words for the chapter or other reading selection and categories in which to place the words. Guessing is encouraged. Then read the selection to see how the words are used in context to support or deny guesses.

→ Example ←

Grades 3-4   Objectives R1, R3, S1, S10

The BFG by Roald Dahl. Farrar, Straus & Giroux, 1982.

ACTIVITY The BFG often gets words mixed up and says words like those listed below. Guess the meaning of each word. Put the letter **P** on the line if you think it is a person; **F** if it is a food and **A** if you think it is an animal. Then listen to the booktalk to support or deny your guesses.

Before		*After*		*Before*		*After*
1. ___ strawbunkles ___				6. ___ cannybull ___		
2. ___ hippodumpling ___				7. ___ childers ___		
3. ___ grocadowndilly ___				8. ___ tottlers ___		
4. ___ snozcumber ___				9. ___ frobscottle ___		
5. ___ human bean ___				10.___ scrumplet ___		

Sophie trembled in fright. Inside the cave it was as dark as night. The giant who had snatched her from her bed gently lowered her to the floor. Suddenly a blaze of light lit up the cavern.

"Please don't eat me," Sophie begged.

"I am not a cannybull," the giant shouted, *"or a hippodumpling or crocadowndilly like you have in your zoo. They eat anything. I only eat snozcumbers."*

"Why did you steal me out of my bed?" Sophie asked.

"Because, you poor little scrumplet, you saw me out of your window. You would have told everyone that giants exist. We simply can't have that so you will just have to stay with me for the rest of your life. Don't worry, I'll protect you from the bad giants."

"What bad giants?" Sophie asked.

"The ones that eat little tottlers," said the BFG. *"Human beans and especially little childers is like strawbunkles and cream to those giants. Here, have a nice drink of frobscottle."*

The more Sophie learns about the other horrible giants who guzzle little childers all over the world, the more she is determined to stop their guzzling. With the help of the BFG who collects dreams in bottles, the Queen of England and the Royal Air Force, Sophie cooks up and carries out her plan. To find out how it all happens, read **The BFG!**

➔ Example ←

Grades 5-6   Objectives R1, R3, S1, S10

Sarah Bishop by Scott O'Dell. Houghton-Mifflin, 1980.

ACTIVITY Use these numbered categories:

1 things needed for wilderness survival
2 loyal to King George
3 patriots
4 food
5 does not fit categories 1-4

Before each word below write the number of the category in which it belongs. Guess if you do not know the word. Then read the book talk on the next page about Sarah Bishop and support or deny your choices.

____ musket	____ Tory	____ vermin	____ pelt
____ maize	____ Skinners	____ tallow	____ chowder
____ Quaker	____ Russet	____ sinew	____ firelock

© Nancy Polette

📖 BOOKTALK

My name is Sarah Bishop. I am a fugitive running from the roar of the muskets and firelocks. I see our home aflame and our barn burning. The Skinners did their work well. Not so much as a chowder bowl was left in the blackened ashes. My father paid with his life for his Tory beliefs. Yet it was the British who accused me of setting the fire and who would have taken me prisoner had I not escaped.

I ration my small store of Russets and maize which must last the winter. I carefully store the gunpowder, molasses, salt and tea bought at the Quaker store before my exile, keeping them hidden from the vermin that share my shelter. I shall survive the coming winter. My light is deer tallow, my bed, fur pelts, my food is mostly fish caught on lines made of deer sinews. Yes, with the coming snows I shall be fed and warm, but nothing made by either man or nature will ever again warm my heart.

Strategy Two: Brainstorming

List as many ideas as possible. All ideas are accepted initially. This strategy pulls from students' experiences and helps to focus on the topics to be covered.

➔ Example ⬅

Grades 3-4   Objectives R1, S1, S12

<u>Heidi</u> by Johanna Spryi. Grosset & Dunlap, 1945.

📖 BOOKTALK

<u>Heidi</u> is a story of the mountains and the girl who found love, happiness and home in her life in the Swiss Alps.

It is only after Heidi is transplanted to city life that she experiences the agony of home-

sickness and the yearning to return to her mountain home. She misses her beloved grandfather who is the only family she has. She misses her good friend Peter and the old, blind Grannie who lived alone in her mountain hut. Who would care for Grannie now that Heidi had gone to the city? But above all, she misses the very sight of the majestic peaks and the spacious blue skies surrounding them.

Heidi dreamed and longed for home, but how could she leave the sick and crippled little girl, Clara, who depended on her? The story is filled with happiness and sorrow.

ACTIVITY Everyone is awed at the sight of tall, majestic mountain ranges, but mountains serve many uses in addition to providing us with spectacular scenery.

Work in groups of two or four, and list as many things as you can that make mountains important to us. Then add to your list by doing some research.

1. create rain forests   6. _____

2. _____   7. _____

3. _____   8. _____

4. ski slopes   9. _____

5. _____   10. provide silver

→ Example ←

Grades 5-6   Objectives R1, S12

ACTIVITY Brainstorm all the hardships and dangers one might face in traveling from London to Boston on a sailing ship in 1832. Then read the booktalk for:

The True Confessions of Charlotte Doyle by Avi. Orchard Books, 1996.

📖 **BOOKTALK**

The year was 1832 when 13-year-old Charlotte Doyle discovered she was the only passenger on the Seahawk setting sail from Liverpool, England, to Providence, Rhode Island.

With quite a bit of nervousness Charlotte boarded the ship and was lead down the steerage to her cabin. She was astonished to find it so small, dark, and inhabited by crawly things. Once in her cabin and alone she groped around in the darkness until she became familiar with its contents. A visit by the ship's cook who warned her of the cruelty of the Captain and gave her a knife for protection did little to calm her fears.

Charlotte succumbed to seasickness and she slept fitfully for what seemed like days. When she awoke she desperately needed air. Once on deck the wind that had before whipped around her was gone. The air held still. She saw a crewman scouring the deck near the gunwale and another out on the bowsprit lurching his way toward the jib boom.

As of this moment Charlotte's life would never be the same. She would see a man whipped and flogged and she herself would be accused of murder. Charlotte bravely promised herself she would not succumb to her feelings of despair. She would survive this voyage and all its horrors. To find out how Charlotte bravely lives through this perilous journey read <u>The True Confessions Of Charlotte Doyle</u>.

Strategy Three: Introducing Vocabulary

→ Example ←

<u>Grades 3-4</u>   <u>Objectives R2, R5, R6, S1, S5, S7</u>

<u>Dakota Dugout</u> by Ann Turner. Macmillan, 1985.

📖 BOOKTALK

We feel the apprehension of the woman narrator as she boards the train in the city to travel across the country to join her husband on the prairie. We experience her shock as she views her first home, a sod house built into the side of the earth. We shiver as snakes drop on her bed at night and as the winter winds blow through the cracks of the hut. We live through the disappointment of a failed summer crop that meant a better life for the couple and despair with them as 12 of their herd of cattle die in a winter storm. We understand the lonely life of the woman as she talks to the sparrows and we understand too, when life does become better and the couple finally manages to build a modern clapboard house, that there are times she misses that first prairie home.

ACTIVITY Study the illustration on the next page. Working in small groups, ask students to write words related to the visual. Have them write on a separate piece of paper. Encourage students to take turns and write nouns, verbs, adjectives and adverbs. After 20 minutes have students use their word banks to create a topic sentence and detailed sentences about the picture. Noun determiners *a, an, the* can be added as well as needed prepositions. This activity can also be done using an illustration from the social studies textbook after reading the chapter.

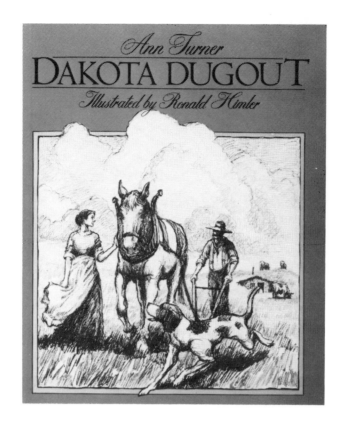

Nouns	Verbs	Adjectives	Adverbs
_____	_____	_____	_____
_____	_____	_____	_____
_____	_____	_____	_____
_____	_____	_____	_____
_____	_____	_____	_____
_____	_____	_____	_____
_____	_____	_____	_____

Jacket illustration for <u>Dakota Dugout</u> 1985 by Ronald Himler, courtesy Macmillan Publishers.

© Nancy Polette

➔Example⬅

Grades 5-6   Objectives R2, R5, R6, S2, S7

Beyond The Western Sea: Book One by Avi. Orchard Books, 1996.

📖 BOOKTALK

It is 1851. An Irish mother and her two children see their home burned and their land devastated by famine. Their only chance for survival is to attempt to join the children's father in America. At the same time, eleven-year-old Sir Laurence Kirkle runs away from home and decides also to go to America. But how will these travelers make such a journey with no food and no money? Was escaping from home really the best idea? At one point in the novel, Laurence is lost in the dark streets of London.

ACTIVITY Choose one of the columns of words from the novel and use ALL of the words in the column to describe the picture of a London street.

devastated	misfortune	distinguished
hostile	constable	congenial
blighted	consultation	proclaim
prosperous	remorse	Hibernian
insurrection	trepidation	composure
interrogation	famine	pandemonium
cowering	mockery	agitated
indignation	scrutinize	scoundrel

Strategy Four: Pre Reading Journals

Provide students with open-ended sentence starters for the story or novel to be read. Relate them in general to the selection. Students choose one sentence starter to write about for five minutes. At the end of the writing time students share orally with small groups what they have written.

→ Example ←

Grades 3-4   Objectives R1, R6, S3, S7

The Iron Giant by Ted Hughes. Knops, 1999.

📖 BOOKTALK

This tale takes place in five nights and tells of an iron giant who is at first feared by the farmers whose land he walks. They lure him into a pit and cover him up but he emerges again in the spring. By that time the entire world is threatened by a strange creature from outer space and the governments of the world unite in attempting to eliminate the creature. Their weapons are to no avail until the Iron Giant steps in to save the world.

ACTIVITY Sample Sentence Starters

Chapter One

1. A story that begins on a high cliff overlooking a deserted beach might be about . . .
2. From a distance, a pile of scrap metal might be mistaken for . . .
3. A small community sometimes does not welcome strangers because . . .

Chapter Two

1. When children report fantastic things they have seen . . .
2. Capturing a dangerous person can be . . .
3. People who at first appear frightening can often . . .

Chapter Three

1. A voracious appetite can lead to . . .
2. Peaceful solutions are best when . . .
3. Happiness for a robot would be . . .

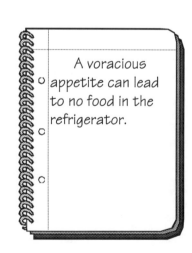

A voracious appetite can lead to no food in the refrigerator.

Chapter Four

1. Humans regard creatures from space as . . .
2. If a person's every demand is instantly satisfied, that person will . . .
3. An example of an even contest is . . .

→Example←

Grades 5-6   Objectives R1, R6, S3, S7

The House of Dies Drear by Virginia Hamilton. Macmillan, 1968.

📖 BOOKTALK

The Small family leases an old Ohio house reportedly haunted by the runaway slaves who died there during the days of the Underground Railroad. Thomas Small, the son, is afraid of and resents old Pluto, the caretaker. Strange shapes appear at night and warning signs are left on doors. The family is not welcomed in the community and Thomas becomes more and more unhappy. Then a series of events leads to the discovery of a treasure trove deep in an underground cave guarded for many years by Pluto.

The Darrow boys want to run Pluto out and get the treasure for themselves. Pluto's son, with the help of the Smalls, foils their plan and the House of Dies Drear finally gives up its secrets.

ACTIVITY Sample Open-ended Sentence Starters from **The House of Dies Drear:**

Chapters One and Two
1. Moving to a new home in a new community . . .
2. People are sometimes wrongly judged by their appearance . . .
3. Many old homes have ghost legends because . . .
4. Asking questions that irritate your parents . . .

Chapters Three and Four
1. A haunted house would look like . . .
2. Looking after younger brothers can be . . .
3. When strange children seem to be making fun of you . . .
4. Secret passageways are fun to explore if . . .

A haunted house would look like it had been mysteriously abandoned decades ago.

Chapters Five and Six
1. When parents think you are making up a story . . .
2. It's not a good idea to rely on first impressions because . . .
3. Waking a person suddenly from sleep . . .
4. A wild man might look like . . .

Chapters Seven and Eight

1. Trying to hide your feelings is not always easy . . .
2. It's hard to tell if someone is telling the truth when . . .
3. When a person appears to be haunted . . .
4. Ghostly figures moving at night . . .

Chapters Nine and Ten

1. Things always seem better in the morning because . . .
2. Strange noises made by air currents can be . . .
3. Going to church on Sunday is . . .
4. When people of the town don't welcome newcomers . . .

Chapters Eleven and Twelve

1. When bad things don't change . . .
2. Ignoring a warning sign can lead to . . .
3. When townsfolk shun one particular family . . .
4. Making friends in a new place is not always easy . . .

Chapters Thirteen and Fourteen

1. Exploring the woods at night . . .
2. When someone just seems to disappear . . .
3. A cave can make a good home for . . .
4. When you think you are seeing double . . .

Chapters Fifteen and Sixteen

1. Ways to tell an imposter . . .
2. Hate can destroy . . .
3. Protecting history and a legend can lead to . . .
4. When a poor man won't touch a treasure . . .

Chapters Seventeen, Eighteen and Nineteen

1. Things a family of rascals might do . . .
2. To really frighten someone . . .
3. To leave something you love seems strange if. . .
4. When one has all the time in the world . . .

A cave can make a good home for furry animals in the hot summer.

Strategy Five: Word Webbing

Write a list of key words from the story or text on the board. Challenge groups or partners to match as many words as they can by drawing a line between two words that are related. The relationship must be identified and explained to the group or class.

→ Example ←

Grades 3-4   Objectives R3, S1, S3, S9

The Hundred Dresses by Eleanor Estes. Harcourt, 1941.

📖 BOOKTALK

Wanda wore the same faded blue dress to school every day. It was always clean but sometimes it looked as though it had been washed and never ironed. Peggy started the game of the dresses when suddenly one day Wanda said, *"I have a hundred dresses at home-all lined up in my closet."* After that it was fun to stop Wanda on the way to school and ask, *"How many dresses did you say you have?"*

"A hundred," she would answer. Then everyone laughed and Wanda's lips would tighten as she walked off with one shoulder hunched up in a way none of the girls understood. Wanda did have the hundred dresses, and this is the story of how Peggy and Maddie came to understand about them and about what their game had meant to Wanda.

ACTIVITY Web these words from The Hundred Dresses:

teacher	popular	precarious
unison	disgraceful	scurry
surrounded	disperse	hundred
incredulous	exaggerated	inseparable
teasing	cruel	hesitate
fringe	enveloped	absent-minded
courage	target	disguise
exquisite	deliberate	thoughtless
intruder	entertainment	admiration

→ Example ←

Grades 5-6   Objectives R3, S1, S3, S9

Escape From Slavery: Five Journeys To Freedom by Doreen Rappaport. Illustrated by Charles Lilly. HarperCollins, 1991.

📖 BOOKTALK

Eliza was stunned to hear the master's words. She was to be sold and separated from her two-year-old daughter, Caroline. She knew what she had to do. Late that night she wrapped Caroline in a blanket and tiptoed out of the cabin, the night air biting her face.

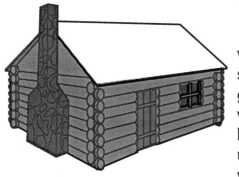

Through the night she walked in the icy air through the woods to the river . . . the river that separated the slave state of Kentucky from the free state of Ohio. The frozen ground bit through her thin shoes, yet the frozen river would be even colder and more dangerous to cross. Just before daylight she reached the river. The ice had broken up. She would have to hide and wait for the cold night wind to freeze the water once again. The baby cried out.

"Shush," Eliza said. *"The slave hunters will hear!"*
Then Eliza spotted a small cabin in the distance. She had heard that some colored folks who lived along the river would help runaways. She looked around. There was no other place to hide. Caroline would not survive the freezing cold for a day. The trackers would soon be there. Eliza had no way of knowing who lived in the cabin as she raised her hand and knocked gently on the door.

ACTIVITY Web these words dealing with the Underground Railroad:

slavery	bondage	Canada	
hardships	waterways	fugitive	
conductor	runaway	masters	
South	buggy	hazards	
station	constitution	newspaper	canon
auction	plantation	price	Civil War
platform	hammer	freedom	cotton
stars	gourd	danger	fields
riders	safe house	track	trapdoor
farmer	Ohio River	Quaker	wagon
signal	Lake Erie	steamship	

© Nancy Polette

Strategy Six: Topic Talking

Assign partners. Partner A speaks to partner B about a topic given by the teacher (and related to the selection to be read) for 10 seconds. The teacher then says switch and B speaks to A on the topic for 10 seconds. The teacher says stop and then gives a second topic. The same procedure is followed but speaking time can be increased. Over a period of weeks, gradually increase the size of the group so that one child is speaking to two others, then three others, etc. Purpose: To get students to share experiences about what they will be reading and to develop oral language facility.

→Example←

Grades 3-4   Objectives R8, S1, S7

Exploring the Environment with **Rabbit Hill** by Robert Lawson. Viking, 1972.

ACTIVITY Follow Strategy Six directions.

Topics   1. a farm   2. an injured animal   3. protecting wildlife

📖 BOOKTALK

Rabbit Hill is a story about the lives of woodland animals. The animals are both excited and concerned because new folks have moved into the big house on Rabbit Hill and it remains to be seen whether they will be friendly or not.

There have been no planting folk residing there in years. The animals are also worried about Porkey, a fat woodchuck, who refuses to move his home which is next to the big house. If the new folks have a dog, Porkey will be in big trouble.

The new folks do arrive and are friendly until one night Little Georgie, a young rabbit, is hit by a car. He is carried into the big house and the animals wonder if they will ever see him again.

<u>Grades 5-6</u>   <u>Objectives R8, S1, S9</u>

<u>The Great Brain</u> by John Fitzgerald. Doubleday, 1967.

ACTIVITY Follow Strategy Six directions.

    Topics   1. a bully   2. the brain   3. making money

📖   **BOOKTALK**

The Great Brain of Adenville, Utah, is Tom. His great brain is always at work, outwitting his friends, his family, the citizens of Adenville and even the Adenville School Board. Tom saves the Jensen brothers from death, fights the meanest bullies, and is always looking for a way to make a profit. When Mr. Standish, the mean school master, crosses the Great Brain, Tom puts his mind to work to devise a devilish scheme. The results are surprising.

➜Example⬅

<u>**Redwall**</u> by Brian Jacques. Philomel, 1983.

ACTIVITY Follow Strategy Six directions.

    Topics   1. the Middle Ages   2. a battle-seasoned horde   3. a hero

📖   **BOOKTALK**

It is the Summer of the Late Rose. But a sinister shadow has fallen across the ancient stone abbey of Redwall, even as the gentle mice of Mossflower Wood gather there to celebrate a year of peace and abundance. For it is rumored that Cluny is coming - Cluny, the terrible one-eyed rat and his battle-seasoned horde. Cluny, whose vow is to conquer Redwall Abbey!

The woodland creatures rush to a desperate defense. But what can an abbey of peace loving mice do against Cluny the Scourge and his army of rats? If only they had the sword of Martin the Warrior, they might have a chance of saving their beloved Abbey. But the hiding place of the legendary sword has been long forgotten, even by the wise old mouse Methuselah. It is his bumbling young apprentice Matthias who sets out to find the sword and who becomes a most unlikely hero.

Strategy Seven: What's Your Opinion?

The teacher lists six to eight statements or commonly held beliefs related to the selection to be read. Working in small groups students write *yes* or *no* indicating their agreement or disagreement with each statement. After reading the selection they again rate the statements *yes* or *no*.

→ Example ←

Grades 3-4   Objectives R1, R2, R3, S1, S7

ACTIVITY Follow the directions in Strategy Seven.

Before   After

_____Black bears like to stand on their heads. _____

_____Black bears often beg for food by holding out their forepaws. _____

_____Black bears are the smallest North American bears. _____

_____A full grown black bear weighs between 250 and 300 pounds. _____

_____Black bears can run fast. _____

_____Black bears can climb trees. _____

_____Black bears sleep in caves in the winter. _____

_____Black bears live 15 to 25 years. _____

The Bears on Hemlock Mountain by Alice Dalgliesh. Macmillan, 1990.

📖 BOOKTALK

Jonathan lived in a stone farmhouse at the foot of Hemlock Mountain. Grown-ups did not think there were bears on the mountain but Jonathan did. Besides, Uncle James said he had once seen a bear.

When Jonathan's mother sent him over the mountain to borrow a large cooking pot from his aunt, the boy is late in returning and a search party goes out looking for him. What they find is a surprise for everyone.

The bears on Hemlock Mountain were probably black bears, sometimes called the clowns of the woods because of their amusing antics, such as standing on their heads, dancing, falling over and over, or begging food with their forepaws stretched out. Black bears are the smallest of North American bears. Their average weight is between 250 and 300 pounds. They can run fast, are good tree climbers and spend the winter sleeping in caves or hollow trees. They live from 15 to 25 years.

→ Example ←

Grades 5-6   Objectives R1, R2, R3, S1, S7

ACTIVITY Give your opinions about life long ago. Answer yes or no.

Before   After

_____ A prince is always well behaved in public.   _____

_____ Living in a palace would be fun.   _____

_____ A young prince cannot be spanked.   _____

_____ An orphan taken to a palace to live would be pleased. _____

_____ Prisoners always want to escape.   _____

_____ It is possible to meet a tame bear in the woods.   _____

The Whipping Boy by Sid Fleischman. Greenwillow Books, 1986.

📖 BOOKTALK

He is known throughout the land as Prince Brat, a name he justly deserves! In his kingdom it is forbidden to spank the heir to the throne. Yet, Prince Brat is forever misbehaving! So an orphan named Jemmy is plucked from the streets to serve as a whipping boy. When Prince Brat greases the Knight's horses' saddles or doesn't do his homework, it is Jemmy who is whipped.

Jemmy dreams of running away but finds himself saddled with the prince who is a less than desirable companion. Captured by cutthroats, Jemmy plans the prince's rescue, which the prince refuses to accept. He likes the adventure of being a prisoner!

When Jemmy finally convinces the Prince to leave, they encounter many more adventures including meeting a tame bear in the woods and running through rat infested sewers to escape their captors. No matter how great the danger, the two boys survive and the lives of both are changed forever.

Strategy Eight: Topic Focusing

Working in small groups, give students a topic related to a non fiction reading selection. Groups list what they know or what they think they know about the topic. Guessing is encouraged. Then read the selection to support or deny guesses.

→ Example ←

Grades 3-4   Objectives R1, R3, S7, S9

ACTIVITY Working with a partner or small group, decide on the best answer to each of the following questions. Guess if you do not know. Then listen to or read the article about Japan to support or deny your guesses.

1. What is the name of a Japanese utensil used for eating?
    A) bamboo B) pogo C) chopsticks

2. A house made of shoji would be made of
    A) brick B) wood C) paper

3. A good pet in Japan would be a
    A) horse B) dog C) cricket

4. A bonsai is a
    A) small tree B) flower C) fish

5. A kimono is a
    A) doll B) dress C) house

6. A favorite Japanese food is
    A) potatoes B) rice C) carrots

7. What type of money is used in Japan?
    A) yen B) franc C) dollar

8. Which food is often eaten raw?
    A) pork B) fish C) beef

About Japan

Boys and girls in Japan enjoy many of the same activities as boys and girls in the United States. They like to play baseball, go to the beach for picnics and watch television.

They eat with a spoon and with chopsticks and especially like rice and raw fish. They usually can't have a puppy in the house because it would tear the shoji or paper doors or dig up the tiny bonsai trees. A Japanese child who had saved enough yen to buy a pet might buy a cricket and cricket cage or a goldfish. On special occasions the girls wear dresses called kimonos.

(Share with the class <u>The Cat Who Went To Heaven</u> by Elizabeth Coatsworth. Macmillan, 1958. It is the tale of a Japanese artist and his cat, Good Fortune.)

➜ Example ⬅

Grades 5-6   Objectives R1, R3, S7, S9

ACTIVITY Working in a small group, answer these questions about the Battle of Britain. Guess if you do not know. Then support or deny your guesses by reading the article that follows.

1. What year did the battle begin?
2. What countries were involved?
3. How long did the battle last?
4. What secret weapon did the British have?
5. How many pounds of bombs were dropped?
6. How many German aircraft were lost?

The Battle of Britain

With France's defeat by the Axis powers in 1940, Britain was left with no allies. Hitler boasted he would march into London in two months and ordered his High Command to

plan an invasion of the British Isles. The German Luftwaffe used Junkers, Dorniers and Stuka Dive Bombers to blast the British airfields, ports and convoys. Air raid shelters and blackouts became a part of British life. Royal Air Force pilots flying Spitfires shot down so many German planes that daylight raids were stopped. Then Goering took command of air assaults and switched to night raids. The town of Coventry was completely destroyed in one night. The British used radar, a carefully guarded secret, to track Jerry planes. From Sept. 7, 1940, to May 11, 1941, the Germans, using incendiary bombs, blasted London nightly. The Home Guard put out fires, transported wounded in lorries and served as air raid wardens. During the Blitz more than 190,000 pounds of bombs were dropped, and German aircraft losses totaled more than 2,600 planes.

(For an exciting novel set in this time in history, read <u>Blitzcat</u> by Robert Westall. Scholastic, 1989.)

© Nancy Polette

Strategy Nine: Find Someone Who . . .

List statements related in general to the literature to be shared. Each student tries to find a different classmate who fits the statement. This is an excellent way to help students see what they have in common with those who lived in a different time or place.

→ Example ←

Grades 3-4   Objectives R4, R8, S3, S5, S7

ACTIVITY Find Someone Who . . .

1. Has ridden on a train. _____

2. Can find Minnesota on a map. _____

3. Has lived a long way from the nearest neighbor. _____

4. Knows what a homestead is. _____

5. Has moved more than one time. _____

6. Who knows what a surveyor does. _____

7. Has helped a family member build a house. _____

8. Likes spring better than the other seasons. _____

By the Shores of Silver Lake by Laura Ingalls Wilder. Harper, 1939.

📖 BOOKTALK

In the days of the building of the railroads and the final settlement of the West the Ingalls family moved from Minnesota, the scene of On the Banks of Plum Creek, to Dakota Territory. Pa became a railroad man for a time until he found a homestead and filed a claim. The family spent the winter in a surveyor's house 60 miles from the nearest neighbor. There was excitement when Laura and Mary took a thrilling train ride and when the attempted payroll robbery took place. That winter the family spent their happiest Christmas ever. In the Spring Pa put up the first building on the town-site near his claim, and two weeks later there was a brand-new town.

Grades 5-6   Objectives R4, R8, S3, S5, S7

ACTIVITY Find Someone Who . . .

1. Can find Vancouver on a map. _____

2. Likes to grow plants. _____

3. Can draw a sketch of a bonsai tree. _____

4. Can name the date Pearl Harbor was bombed. _____

5. Has moved from one city to another. _____

6. Has visited or lived in Canada. _____

7. Has been unjustly accused of something. _____

8. Has camped in the mountains. _____

9. Knows what discrimination means. _____

10. Has explored a cave. _____

The Eternal Spring of Mr. Ito by Sheila Garrigue. Bradbury, 1984.

📖 BOOKTALK

Sent from London to live with relatives in Canada during World War Two, young Sara becomes friends with the Japanese gardener, Mr. Ito. He explains the meaning of the bonsai tree to Sara and shows her how to grow her own. Pearl Harbor is attacked and Sara's cousin's fiancee is killed. Her uncle is in charge of rounding up all Japanese and sending them to camps. Mr. Ito takes refuge in an isolated cave, going there to die. As hostility toward the Japanese increases, life at Sara's aunt's becomes tense. Mr. Ito dies and Sara promises to pass his bonsai tree on to his family. But how can she when the camps are far away and anyone helping the Japanese is branded a traitor? Here is the story of a courageous young girl told with the background of real history - a story in which all participants learn the power of understanding.

Strategy Ten: Rank Order

Given a list of items, students rank them from most to least desirable.

→ Example ←

Grades 3-4   Objectives R1, R2, S7, S10

ACTIVITY If you were all alone on a large island, rank these activities from the most difficult to the least difficult. The most difficult item will be first on your list.

Rank Order

Escaping flood waters　　　　　　　　　_____

Finding food　　　　　　　　　　　　　_____

Finding shelter　　　　　　　　　　　　_____

Fighting boredom with no one to talk to　_____

Homesickness　　　　　　　　　　　　　_____

Abel's Island by William Steig. Farrar, Straus & Giroux, 1975.

📖 **BOOKTALK**

Abel's place in his familiar mouse world had always been secure. He had an allowance from his mother, a comfortable home, and a lovely wife, Amanda. But one stormy August day flood waters carry him off and dump him on an uninhabited island.

Using his determination and stubborn resourcefulness, he tries crossing the river with boats and ropes and even on stepping stones. Abel can't find a way to get back home.

Days then weeks and months pass. Slowly his soft habits disappear as he forages for food, fashions a warm nest in a hollow log, models clay statues of his family, and continues to brood on the problem of how to get across the river and back home.

Abel's time on the island brings him a new understanding of the world he is separated from. Faced with the daily adventure of survival in his solitary, somewhat hostile domain, he is moved to reexamine the easy way of life he had always accepted and discovers skills and talents in himself that hold promise of a more meaningful life if and when he should finally return to Mossville and his dear Amanda again.

Grades 5-6   Objectives R1, R2, S7, S10

ACTIVITY If you lived in the Middle Ages here is a list of common professions. Rank order the list from the most desirable (first on your list) to the least desirable.

_____ Painter

_____ Crusader

_____ Maker of songs

_____ Peddler

_____ Minstrel

_____ Monk

_____ Knight

_____ Wart Charmer

Catherine, Called Birdy by Karen Cushman. Clarion Books, 1994.

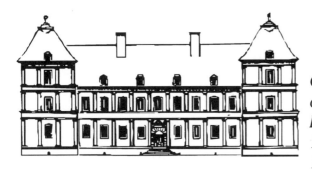

📖 **BOOKTALK**

What follows will be my book, the book of Catherine, called Little Bird or Birdy, daughter of Rollo and the lady Aislinn, sister to Thomas, Edward, and the abominable Robert. Begun this 19th day of September in the year of Our Lord 1290 . . . Picked off 29 fleas today.

Catherine's mother wants to teach her the skills of the lady of the manor and to prepare her to be a gentle and patient wife. Her father wants only to see her married off and profitable. Catherine herself hopes to become a painter, a Crusader, a maker of songs, a peddler, a minstrel, a monk, a wart charmer . . . Of all the possibilities, she has ruled out only one: being sold like a cheese to the highest bidder.

Against a vivid background of everyday life on a medieval English manor, Catherine's earthy, spirited account of her 14th year is a richly entertaining story with an utterly unforgettable heroine.

Strategy Eleven: Critical Listening

A student writes ten clues about a topic. This can be a non fiction topic or a topic dealing with a literary character or setting. A member of the class gives a number. The clue for that number is read. The student can guess the answer or pass. The game continues until the correct answer is given or all clues are read. One clue must be a give away clue.

➔Example⬅

Grades 3-4   Objectives R3, R7, S3, S5, S7

ACTIVITY The Mystery State

1. The state bird is the bluebird.
2. This was the 24th state.
3. This state is 19th in area size among the states.
4. The greatest distance north to south in this state is 335 miles.
5. For many years the state's most important mineral was lead.
6. The capital is Jefferson City.
7. The state has about 10,000 springs.
8. The Clydesdale horses live in this state when not on parade.
9. One of Laura Ingalls Wilder's homes is in this state.
10. The state song is *The Missouri Waltz*.
        (Answer: Missouri)

➔Example⬅

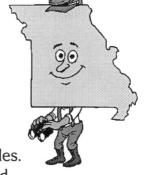

Grades 5-6   Objectives R3, R7, S3, S5, S7

ACTIVITY The Mystery Person

1. This person was born in Virginia.
2. He lived for a time in a frontier settlement in Tennessee.
3. When he was 15 he ran away from home.
4. He was adopted by the Cherokee Indians.
5. He was a school teacher for a time.
6. He led Texas' fight for independence.
7. He served in Andrew Jackson's army in the fight against the Creek Indians.
8. He was severely wounded in battle.
9. He became governor of Tennessee.
10. He was the President of the new Republic of Texas. *(Answer: Sam Houston)*

Strategy Twelve: Critical Reading Skills

A. USING CONTEXT CLUES Understanding words and ideas as they are used in a particular situation.

B. PREDICTING OUTCOMES A critical reader asks: What is the problem? What will happen next? What is the evidence for the prediction? What are other possibilities? How can I find out?

C. IDENTIFYING CAUSE AND EFFECT

D. SEPARATING FACT FROM OPINION A fact is a statement that can be proven. An opinion is what a person thinks about another person or situation and may or may not be true.

→ Example ←

A. USING CONTEXT CLUES Understanding words and ideas as they are used in a particular situation.

Grades 3-4   Objectives R1, R2, R3, S6, S7, S10

Johnny Appleseed by Steven Kellogg. Morrow, 1988.

ACTIVITY Can you tell what a legend is by reading this booktalk?

📖 BOOKTALK

John Chapman, later known as Johnny Appleseed, was born in 1774. He had 10 stepbrothers and stepsisters. When he was old enough he set out to explore the western frontier which at that time was western Pennsylvania. He carried a pouch of appleseeds with him and planted them for future settlers who would live there.

He made friends with the animals and with the Indians. Many legends grew up about him. Steven Kellogg has blended both fact and legend to create a picture of a true tall tale hero.

➜ Example ←

Grades 5-6   Objectives R1, R2, R3, S6, S7, S10

<u>The Boggart</u> by Susan Cooper. Atheneum, 1993.

ACTIVITY What is a Boggart? Your answer must be REASONABLE, based on EVIDENCE and you should be able to cite SUPPORTING DETAILS.

📖 BOOKTALK

In a tumbledown castle in the Western Highlands of Scotland lives the Boggart. He is invisible, an ancient mischievous spirit, solitary and sly, born of a magic as old as the rocks and the waves. He has lived in Castle Keep for centuries, playing tricks on the owners. But the last Scottish owner has died and left the castle to his great-nephew Robert Volnik of Toronto, Canada. The Volnik family, including Emily and her nine-year-old computer-genius brother Jessup, visit Castle Keep, and when they return to Toronto, they unwittingly take the Boggart with them. The astonishment, delights, and horrors that invade their lives with the arrival of the Boggart fill this swiftly moving story. The collision of modern technology and the Old Magic brings perils nobody could have imagined and, in the end, an amazing and touching solution to the problem of the Boggart who has found himself on the wrong side of the ocean.

➜ Example ←

B. PREDICTING OUTCOMES A critical reader asks: What is the problem? What will happen next? What is the evidence for the prediction? What are other possibilities? How can I find out?

Grades 3-4   Objectives R1, R2, R3, S6, S7, S10

<u>Pilgrim</u> by Barbara Cohen. Lothrop, 1983.

ACTIVITY Read the following booktalk. Predict what will happen. What evidence can you give for your prediction?

📖 BOOKTALK

Molly is unhappy in her new school because the children tease her. Her family has come from Russia, and her dress and speech are different from the other children.

Thanksgiving approaches and the teacher asks each child to make a doll - Indians for the boys and Pilgrims for the girls. Molly explains to her mother that a Pilgrim came to this country from the other side for religious freedom. *"Just like us!"* her mother answers.

Mother makes a Pilgrim doll that looks like her. Molly is embarrassed to take the doll to school. She knows the children will laugh. Predict what happens.

→Example←

Grades 5-6   Objectives R1, R2, R3, S6, S7, S10

Mr. Revere And I by Robert Lawson. Little Brown, 1953.

ACTIVITY What evidence can you find that would lead you to believe that Sherry was the horse Paul Revere used on his famous ride?

📖 BOOKTALK

In 1770 Paul Revere was a Boston silversmith. It was a time of turmoil, for the King of England had sent troops to Boston to occupy the port and to uphold the King's decrees. The people of Boston resented the soldiers who had little to do and often spent their days gambling. One officer lost his horse, Sherry, in a card game to a man who owned a glue factory. The new owner treated Sherry so badly that a group of citizens took the horse away and gave it to Paul Revere. Paul had no barn so he housed the horse in a lean-to next to his house and began taking riding lessons. Discover how Sherry becomes a very famous horse, indeed, with her novice rider in Mr. Revere and I.

© Nancy Polette

C. IDENTIFYING CAUSE AND EFFECT

→Example←

Grades 3-4   Objectives R1, R2, R3, S6, S7, S10

<u>Backyard Bear</u> by Jim Murphy. Illustrated by Jeffrey Greene. Scholastic, 1993.

ACTIVITY Read the booktalk that follows. What caused the young bear to wander into the town? What were the effects of this journey?

📖 BOOKTALK

It's a moonlit night when the hungry young bear pauses at the foot of the mountain. To cross the ribbon of asphalt separating his forest from the town below is to trespass. But the delicious smell of food is too inviting and, a second later, he crosses the road and enters the sleeping town. He wanders from one backyard to another going deeper and deeper into a strange and scary world. And when a sudden noise startles the townspeople awake, what had been a harmless search for food becomes a frightening chase. Will the young bear escape the humans who are determined to catch him?

→Example←

Grades 5-6   Objectives R1, R2, R3, S6, S7, S10

<u>Medicine Walk</u> by Ardath Mayhar. Atheneum, 1985.

ACTIVITY What caused the plane to crash? What were the effects of the crash?

📖 BOOKTALK

It was not to be a long flight, the trip to grandfather's. And they had plenty of time. *"Why not fly over the Petrified Forest?"* Burr suggested to his father, who was piloting their small plane. So the two went off their flight plan, and when the accident happened, when Burr's father had a heart attack and died after bringing the plane to a landing in a desert draw, there was no way anyone would know where to look for them.

Burr did not want to leave the plane, did not want to leave his dead father. But no one would ever find him, with the plane at rest under a desert cottonwood tree in an area where they had not intended to be. He had no choice, if he wanted to live, but to take the small amount of water and food aboard the plane, stored there for emergencies, and start over the hot summer desert. There were no roads to follow, no paths, and he would have to walk at least 40 miles.

D. SEPARATING FACT FROM OPINION   A fact is a statement that can be proven. An opinion is what a person thinks about another person or situation and may or may not be true.

→Example←

Grades 3-4   Objectives R1, R2, R3, S6, S7, S10

Fourth Grade Rats by Jerry Spinelli. Scholastic, 1991.

ACTIVITY Find two facts and three opinions in the booktalk.

📖 BOOKTALK

First grade babies! Second grade cats! Third grade angels! Fourth grade rats! Suds wishes he was still in the third grade so he could keep being an angel. But his best friend, Joey, is proud to be a rat, which he calls the next step to being a man. According to Joey, fourth grade rats aren't afraid of spiders, don't carry babyish lunch boxes, and they don't cry. What rats do is push little kids off the swings, say no to their mothers, and eat real meat (like bologna).

Becoming a real rat doesn't sound too good to Suds, who discovers that growing up can sometimes be painful.

→Example←

Grades 5-6   Objectives R1, R2, R3, S6, S7, S10

The Double Life of Pocahontas by Jean Fritz. Putnam's, 1983.

ACTIVITY Find three facts and two opinions in this booktalk.

📖 BOOKTALK

Pocahontas, an Indian princess, daughter of Chief Powhatan, befriends the English settler, John Smith, who is adopted into the tribe. When fire destroys Jamestown, the English settlement, she visits often, bringing food. But a series of poor leaders cause the settlers and the Indians to war with each other. During one winter, most of the settlers starve but more arrive. Hostilities increase and Pocahontas is kidnapped. Christian beliefs are forced on her and she eventually marries an Englishman. Caught between two worlds, she journeys to England with her husband and son where she dies, never resolving the conflict of identity that was her life.

→Example←

Grades 3-4   Objectives R1, R9, S1, S4

In <u>Abel's Island</u> by William Steig, Abel the mouse awakens to find himself wet, hungry and all alone on an island. He makes three tries to get across the river where his home is by building three different boats, but none are successful.

ACTIVITY Think of other ways Abel might get across the river
by completing items 1 to 7.

1. What important facts can you state about the situation?

2. State the major problem.

3. List as many ideas as you can to deal with the problem.

4. Select the four best ideas and enter them on the grid below.

5. Two criteria for judging ideas are provided on the grid. Add a third of your own.

6. Evaluate each idea giving a 1 if no, 2 if maybe and 3 if yes.
   The idea with the highest score is the best idea.

Ideas	?	Fast?	Possible?	Total

7. The best idea is _____

→ Example ←

Grades 5-6   Objectives R1, R9, S1, S4

In <u>Catherine, Called Birdy</u> by Karen Cushman, young Birdy, who lives in the Middle Ages, is to be forced to marry against her will. She ponders how to escape her coming betrothal as negotiations for her marriage continue. A fall wedding is decided upon and days are spent with lessons on being a lady, more arguments with her father and more bruises. How might she escape this fate?

1. What important facts can you state about the situation?

2. State the major problem.

3. List as many ideas as you can to deal with the problem.

4. Select the four best ideas and enter them on the grid below.

5. Two criteria for judging ideas are provided on the grid. Add a third of your own.

6. Evaluate each idea giving a scale of one (poor) to five (good).
   The idea with the highest score is the best idea.

Ideas	Fast?	Possible?	?	Total

7. The best idea is

_____

_____

_____

→ Example ←

Grades 3-4   Objectives R1, R2, R8, S2, S9

Preparing Scripts for Readers Theatre

It is possible to create readers theatre scripts from any form of narrative - a newspaper article, a fable, a paragraph from a social studies or science text, or the jacket blurb of a book. There is no expense involved, no props or costumes are used, and the readers theatre group both prepares and performs its own script. Here is how it is done.

1. Read the piece together with each person reading a line in turn.
2. Decide which characters will speak.
3. Decide which characters will need narrators.
4. Narrator speaking parts can be marked N1 for Narrator One and N2 for Narrator Two. Each narrator reads those lines which apply to his or her character.
5. Words which indicate what a character is thinking, feeling or doing can be spoken by that character. Character parts are indicated with the first letter of the character's name.
6. NO WORDS IN THE SELECTION ARE CHANGED.

Study the sample booktalk that follows to see how it becomes a readers theatre script.

Maya's Children: The Story of La Llorona by Rudolfo Anaya. Illus. by Maria Baca. Hyperion Books, 1996.

📖 **BOOKTALK**

On a night when the wind howled through the trees and the rain cried tears in protest, Maya was born. Her smile was as beautiful as the sunrise but her face was flawed by a strange mark which the village priest knew to be a sign of immortality. As she grew to young womanhood, Maya was kind and loving and extended the hand of friendship to old and young alike. But Maya's gift of immortality drove Senor Tiempo, the god of time, wild with jealousy, for only he had the right to allot to the world's creatures their time on earth. Though he could not control her destiny, Senor Tiempo used his powers to rob Maya of her heart's dearest treasure, her multitude of miraculous children raised from bowlsful of earth. Devastated, Maya wanders the countryside forever wailing for the lost children and is known evermore as La Llorona, the Wailing Woman.

Readers Theatre

<u>Maya's Children: The Story of La Llorona</u> by Rudolfo Anaya. Illus by
Maria Baca. Hyperion Books, 1996.

Reading Parts: Narrator One = N1   Narrator Two = N2
                Maya = M   Senior Tiempo = S

Whole cast makes wind rushing sounds and sound of raindrops falling.

N1: On a night when the wind howled through the trees and the rain cried tears in
      protest, Maya was born. Her smile

M: was as beautiful as the sunrise

N1: but her face

M: was flawed by a strange mark

N2: which the village priest knew to be a sign of immortality.

N1: As she grew to young womanhood, Maya

M: was kind and loving and extended the hand of friendship to old and young alike.

N2: But Maya's gift of immortality drove Senor Tiempo, the god of time,

S: wild with jealousy,

N2: for only he had the right

S: to allot to the world's creatures their time on earth.

N2: Though he could not

S: control her destiny,

N2: Senor Tiempo used his powers

S: to rob Maya of her heart's dearest treasure,

N1: her multitude of miraculous children raised from bowlsful of earth. Devastated,
      Maya

M: wanders the countryside forever wailing for the lost children

N1: and is known evermore as La Llorona, the Wailing Woman.

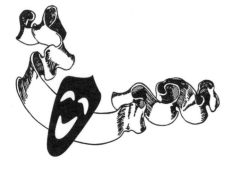

→ Example ←

Grades 5-6   Objectives R1, R2, R8, S2

Transforming Narrative to Dialogue

The Righteous Revenge of Artemis Bonner by Walter Dean Myers. HarperCollins, 1992.

📖 BOOKTALK

In 1880 two important events took place. Catfish Grimes shot dead Ugly Ned Bonner, uncle to Artemis Bonner and Artemis headed west to avenge Uncle Ugly's death and find the gold mine left to him in his uncle's will. Catfish Grimes is determined not to be caught. He would also like to find the gold mine before Artemis does. But Artemis has the strength of TRUE DETERMINATION! He tracks Catfish from Mexico to Alaska and back again. Finally they meet in a shootout in front of the Bird Cage Saloon. Catfish yelled, *"When I count three, go for your gun."* No sooner had he shouted *"One"* than both Catfish and Artemis drew. Read to discover the exciting finish to this romp through the Old West.

Speaking Parts: N1=Narrator One, N2=Narrator Two, A=Artemis, C=Catfish

N1: In 1880 two important events took place.

N2: Catfish Grimes

C: shot dead Ugly Ned Bonner,

N2: uncle to Artemis Bonner and

N1: Artemis

A: headed west to avenge Uncle Ugly's death and find the gold mine

N1: left to him in his uncle's will.

N2: Catfish Grimes

C: is determined not to be caught.

N2: He would also like

C: to find the gold mine before Artemis does.

N1: But Artemis has the strength

A: of TRUE DETERMINATION!

N1: He tracks Catfish

A: from Mexico to Alaska and back again.

N2: Finally they meet in a shootout

N1: in front of the Bird Cage Saloon.

N2: Catfish yelled

C: "When I count three go for your gun."

N2: No sooner had he shouted

C: "One"

N1: than both Catfish and Artemis drew.

N2: Read to discover the exciting finish

N1: to this romp through the Old West.

POST READING STRATEGIES

Strategy Fifteen: Asking Good Questions

→Example←

Grades 3-6   Objectives R1, R2, R3, S1, S9, S11

ACTIVITY Thinking More Deeply About the Reading Selection

Divide the class into four teams. Each team will discuss one of the categories of questions below. A spokesperson for each team will report on the discussion to the class.

Four Levels of Questions

OBJECTIVE
1. What words or phrases do you remember?
2. What people do you remember seeing?
3. What colors, objects, sounds, textures do you recall?

REFLECTIVE
1. Whom did you like or dislike in the story?
2. With whom did you identify?
3. What emotions did you see in the story? When?
4. What kind of music would you choose to accompany this story?

INTERPRETATIVE
1. Was there any point in the story when you felt happy? sad? apprehensive? angry? disappointed?
2. If you could have stopped the story at any point, where would you have stopped it?
3. If you needed to shorten the story, where would you have made the cuts?

DECISIONAL
1. How do you think the main character felt at the end of the story?
2. Have you ever felt like this?
3. Who needs to read this story? (Think of a historical figure or another character from literature.)
4. If you could be any of the characters, which would you choose to be?
5. What title would you give this story?

Strategy Sixteen: Group Discussion Questions

Use these beginnings: How many ways . . . What if . . . If you were . . .
How is ___ like ___? Give each small group one question related to the story.
The group has a recorder to list main ideas while they discuss the question
for 10 minutes.
Example How many ways is <u>Charlotte's Web</u> like the story of Cinderella?

→Example←

Grades 3-4   Objectives R1, R2, R3, S1, S9, S11

<u>**Now Let Me Fly: The Story of a Slave Family**</u> written and illustrated by Delores
Johnson. Macmillan, 1993.

ACTIVITY Read the booktalk. Use the questions that follow in a
small group discussion.

📖 BOOKTALK

When Minna hears the drums reverberating across the broad African Savanna, she asks
her mother, *"Will there be dancing tonight or will the old ones tell their stories?"*
"No, child, there's no joy in the sound of those drums."
And indeed there is not for the drums signal the beginning of a lifelong horror for
Minna. The next day she is kidnapped, forced to march in chains and sold into slavery.
After that comes the agonizing three month voyage to America and only the friendship
offered by a boy her age, Amadi, keeps Minna alive. In America Minna and Amadi are sold
at auction and join other slaves on a large plantation. Eventually they marry and have
children of their own. But their freedom is only a far-off dream.

1. How many ways might Minna have tried to escape from the slavers?
2. If you were Minna how would you have felt never having freedom?
3. Suppose that Minna had escaped after she reached the plantation. What might have
   happened to her?
4. What if slavery had never existed? How might society be different today?
5. In what ways are Minna's story and the fairy tale <u>Rapunzel</u> alike?

Use these beginnings:

> How many ways . . .
> What if . . .
> If you were . . .
> How is _____ like _____?

➔ Example ⬅

Grades 5-6   Objectives R1, R2, R3, S1, S9, S11

Nettie's Trip South by Ann Turner. Macmillan, 1987.

📖 BOOKTALK

As Nettie writes to her friend Addie about her trip from Albany, New York, to Richmond, Virginia, she remembers all the things she saw and heard in that pre-Civil War South. She remembers the sweet cedar smell in the air but she also remembers Tabitha, the black slave in her hotel, who has no last name. She remembers seeing the slave quarters at a nearby plantation, with the heaps of rags in the corners for beds. But most of all she remembers the slave auction, where a woman is sold like a sack of flour; and she thinks about what their lives would be like if she and Addie were slaves. Based on the real diary of the author's great-grandmother, this is a powerful and deeply moving account of one girl's reaction to slavery in the South. Once read and seen through the eyes of master illustrator Ronald Himler, it is not soon forgotten.

ACTIVITY In what way or ways are any of these headlines related to this book?

OPEC INCREASES OIL PRICES

NEW WELFARE LAW PASSED

PRISON OVERCROWDING A PROBLEM

DRUG RAID A SUCCESS

UNITED FUND TOPS GOAL

Strategy Seventeen: Graphic Organizers

A. Story Mapping
B. Emotion Chart
C. The Venn Diagram

→Example←

A. Story Mapping

Grades 3-4   Objectives R2, R9, S1, S10

<u>Shoeshine Girl</u> by Clyde Robert Bulla. Crowell, 1975.

📖 BOOKTALK

Ten-and-a-half-year-old Sarah Ida is angry about spending the summer at Aunt Claudia's. She has been sent away because her parents can't cope with her. Not only that, her best friend has been caught stealing for kicks.

Money in her pocket is Sarah Ida's symbol of independence. When Aunt Claudia says no allowance, Sarah Ida is determined to get even and find a job. The shoeshine stand is the only place that will hire a ten-year-old girl. To Sarah Ida's surprise Aunt Claudia doesn't object. And that is only the first of many surprises the summer holds for her.

ACTIVITY Complete the Story Mapping for <u>Shoeshine Girl</u>.

CHARACTERS	SETTING
EVENTS	
PROBLEM	
EVENTS	
GOAL	

© Nancy Polette

B. Emotion Chart

➔Example←

Shadow of a Bull by Maia Wojciechowska. Atheneum, 1964.

📖 BOOKTALK

Olivar was the son of his father which may not seem like a necessary thing to say. But in Manolo's case it is. For his father had been Juan Olivar, the greatest bullfighter in all Spain, and Manolo was his son in two special ways: one, he looked just like his father; and two, everyone expected that he, Manolo Olivar, would repeat the success of his father, would be just what his father had been, a fighter of bulls and a killer of death.

No one asked Manolo if his future was his choice. He had no choice. And only he knew that the bullfighter's unconquerable urge to fight bulls was not a part of him.

The day was chosen and the bull selected for the fight that would establish Manolo's future. Caught in a web not of his making, Manolo struggles to retain his pride, his self-respect, and the independence that goes far beyond the world of bullfighters and the borders of Spain. These are the struggles of every boy in the process of becoming a man.

ACTIVITY Complete this emotion chart for Manolo in **Shadow of a Bull**.

THE EMOTION IS *FEAR*

High Intensity

Low Intensity

Beginning   Middle   End

C. The Venn Diagram

→Example←

__The Serpent Never Sleeps__ by Scott O'Dell. Houghton-Mifflin, 1975.

📖 **BOOKTALK**

Serena Lynn, age seventeen, is asked by England's King, James I, to serve at court. She is very pleased, but must decline: she is loyal to the man she's always loved, Anthony Foxcroft. Anthony is embroiled in disputes at court and must ship out for Jamestown, the first colony in the New World. Serena will go too.

They sail on the *Sea Venture*, which leaves Plymouth, England, in 1609 to take supplies and more settlers to Virginia. Their small boat seems no match for the wild sea, but they are spared only to be shipwrecked off Bermuda. The brave crew builds a new boat so their expedition can flounder on to Virginia.

When they arrive, Jamestown is in ruins. Those who have survived the deadly winter are in desperate need of food. The Indians, with whom the colonists have maintained a delicate peace, may be their only chance. Serena goes with a party sent to plead with Pocahontas, the Indian princess who saved them once before, and who may have the power to save them again.

ACTIVITY Use the Venn Diagram to compare Serena and Pocahontas.

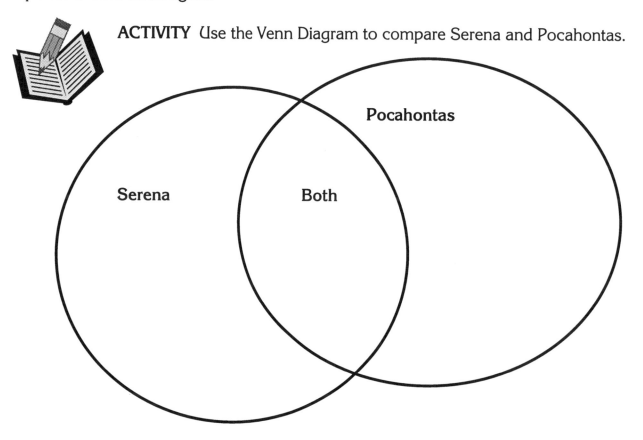

© Nancy Polette CLC0223 Pieces of Learning

→Example←

Grades 3-6   Objectives R6, R9, S1, S10

<u>Nouns</u> . . . can be . . . common, proper,
. . . singular, plural,
. . . possessive, collective.

ACTIVITY From any selection find and read aloud the following kinds of sentences.

A sentence that contains . . .

1. Both a *common* noun and a *proper* noun.

2. A singular noun which has been made *plural* by adding **s**.

3. A singular noun which has been made *plural* by adding **es**.

4. A *possessive* noun.

5. A *plural* noun.

ACTIVITY Write a sentence describing a character. This sentence must contain a singular noun, a plural noun, a proper noun, a possessive noun, two adjectives and a verb.

Prefixes and Suffixes
A PREFIX is letters added to the beginning of a word to change the meaning.
an, de, dis, il, in, non, and *un* mean **not**
after, ante, pre and *pro* mean **when**
on, off, under, pro and *sub* mean **where**

A SUFFIX is letters added to the end of a word.
Some suffixes added to **nouns** are *ant, ent, er, ess, or, cy, ism*
Some suffixes added to **adjectives** are *ful, ous, less, er, est, ble*
Some suffixes added to **adverbs** are *ily, ly, ways, ise*
Some suffixes added to **verbs** are *ed, ing, en, fy*

ACTIVITY From any selection find and read aloud a sentence that contains words with both a prefix and a suffix. Find and read aloud sentences which contain words with any prefix or suffix listed above.

ACTIVITY Have a Sentence Treasure Hunt

Choose teams of three. All teams are looking at the same text. When the signal to begin is given, teams search for the ten items below. The team finding the most sentences in the time given is the winner.

1. A sentence that shows regret.

_____

2. A sentence with two noun clauses.

_____

3. A sentence that contains both a concrete and an abstract noun.

_____

4. A sentence with a possessive proper noun and a singular common noun.

_____

5. An imperative sentence.

_____

6. A sentence with an adverb that tells how.

_____

7. A sentence with two prepositional phrases.

_____

8. A sentence with seven nouns and two pronouns.

_____

9. A sentence that contains a homophone or a homograph.

_____

10. A sentence that contains an idiom.

_____

Literary Style

Read the definitions below for the tools of the writer's trade. Summarize a novel in seven sentences but follow the directions for what each of your sentences must contain.

Alliteration Repeating beginning sounds *(Peter Piper picked)*

Personification Giving life to non living objects *(Fingers of wind plucked the clothes)*

Hyperbole Absurd exaggeration, doing something to excess *(Davy Crockett killed a bear when he was only three.)*

Repetition Repeating phrases for emphasis *(His right foot, his enormous right foot, lifted up and out)*

Imagery Use of the senses in describing *(taste, smell, touch, sight, hearing)*

Simile Comparisons using like or as *(As neat as a pin)*

Metaphor Comparing without the use of like or as *(The sea was a cauldron)*

1. A sentence that contains a *simile.*

_____

2. A sentence that contains *alliteration.*

_____

3. A sentence which contains *hyperbole.*

_____

4. A sentence with good *imagery.*

_____

5. A sentence that contains a *metaphor.*

_____

6. A sentence that uses *repetition* for effect.

_____

7. A sentence that shows *personification.*

_____

Similes

List 10 persons, places or objects from the selection that has been read.

_____   _____

_____   _____

_____   _____

_____   _____

_____   _____

Describe the 10 things you listed using any one of the similes below.

1. As fat as a _____   Describes _____

2. As light as a _____   Describes _____

3. As cold as _____   Describes _____

4. As lovely as _____   Describes _____

5. As smooth as _____   Describes _____

6. As hard as a _____   Describes _____

7. As soft as _____   Describes _____

8. As strong as _____   Describes _____

9. As worn as _____   Describes _____

10. As dark as _____   Describes _____

11. As busy as _____   Describes _____

12. As happy as _____   Describes _____

13. As hungry as _____   Describes _____

14. As sweet as _____   Describes _____

15. As quiet as _____   Describes _____

16. As stubborn as _____   Describes _____

17. As tall as _____   Describes _____

18. As thin as _____   Describes _____

19. As loud as _____   Describes _____

20. As rough as _____   Describes _____

Idioms

Idioms are colorful words used to convey a description or an idea. The words do not actually mean what they say. For example: *"We're in hot water"* has nothing to do with water. It simply means *"We're in trouble."*

Choose four of the common idioms listed below. Who in the novel would have used the idiom and when?

Stop pulling my leg.

It's just chicken feed.

That's the way the cookie crumbles.

Go fly a kite.

He has a green thumb.

Get off my back!

He's out on his ear.

Button your lip.

Keep a stiff upper lip.

It's a dog's life.

We're up a creek.

It's in the bag.

Cat got your tongue?

It's raining cats and dogs.

You've hit it on the button.

Drop me a line.

Get out of my hair.

We're all in the same boat.

You really put your foot in your mouth this time.

1. (Character) _____ would have said (idiom) _____

_____

to or about _____

_____

when _____.

2. (Character) _____ would have said (idiom) _____

_____

to or about _____

_____

when _____.

3. (Character) _____ would have said (idiom) _____

_____

to or about _____

_____

when _____.

4. (Character) _____ would have said (idiom) _____

_____

to or about _____

_____

when _____.

Confusing Words

Because some words seem alike in some ways, these words are often used incorrectly. Study the words and their meanings. Write four sentences about the characters, setting or situations in the book you have read using one pair of words in each sentence.

ascent (go up)	assent (consent)
accept (agree)	except (excluding)
affect (to influence)	effect (result)
bizarre (odd)	bazaar (market/fair)
command (order)	commend (praise)
conscience (sense of right)	conscious (awake)
contagious (catching)	contiguous (nearby)
credible (believable)	creditable (deserving praise)
desert (arid land)	dessert (ice cream)
elicit (to draw out)	illicit (unlawful)
emigrate (to leave)	immigrate (to enter)
indigent (needy)	indignant (angry)
perpetrate (to commit)	perpetuate (ongoing)
personal (private)	personnel (body of people)
quiet (not noisy)	quite (very)
recent (not long ago)	resent (to feel indignant)

Example Caddie Woodlawn did not ACCEPT the fact that she should be a young lady EXCEPT when her mother was present.

1. _____

_____

2. _____

_____

3. _____

_____

4. _____

_____

Homographs

Homographs are words that are spelled the same but have different meanings.

Example: It was *fine* with me that he had to pay the *fine*.

arms (body parts)   date (day, year)   jar (container)
arms (weapons)   date (fruit)   jar (rattle)

ball (dance)   down (move lower)   lean (stand slanting)
ball (round object)   down (feathers)   lean (not fat)

bark (tree covering)   duck (bird)   lock (fasten door)
bark (sound of a dog)   duck (lower suddenly)   lock (hair)

bat (club)   fair (pretty)   miss (fail to hit)
bat (mammal)   fair (just)   miss (unmarried girl)

bear (animal)   fast (speedy)   mum (silent)
bear (carry)   fast (go without food) mum (flower)

can (able to)   fly (insect)   pitcher (container)
can (container)   fly (with wings)   pitcher (baseball player)

clip (cut)   grave (burial)   seal (close)
clip (fasten)   grave (serious)   seal (mammal)

content (things inside) ground (soil)   sock (to hit)
content (satisfied)   ground (did grind)   sock (foot covering)

count (1, 2, 3)   hide (conceal)   steer (guide)
count (nobleman)   hide (animal skin)   steer (male cattle)

OR

© Nancy Polette   CLC0223 Pieces of Learning

Choose from the pairs of homographs on page 58. Write sentences about a character or the setting from the novel you have read using a pair of homographs in each sentence.

1. _____

_____

2. _____

_____

3. _____

_____

4. _____

_____

5. _____

_____

6. _____

_____

7. _____

_____

8. _____

_____

9. _____

_____

10. _____

_____

→ Example ←

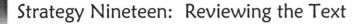

Grades 3-6   Objectives R1, R2, R3, S2, S5

ACTIVITY Cut apart the cards on this page labeled locations, occupations, times, feelings and problems. Working in teams, each team receives one card. The team that finds the most examples in the book in a given time period is the winner. Items found can be those that are specifically stated or inferred.

LOCATIONS

OCCUPATIONS

TIMES

FEELINGS

PROBLEMS

© Nancy Polette

Strategy Twenty: Cause and Effect

→ Example ←

Grades 3-4   Objectives R2, R3, R4, S5, S6, S10

<u>Mr. Revere and I</u> by Robert Lawson. Little-Brown, 1953.

ACTIVITY Complete the cause and effect statements that follow.

📖 BOOKTALK

In 1770 Paul Revere was a Boston silversmith. It was a time of turmoil for the King of England had sent troops to Boston to occupy the port and to uphold the King's decrees. The people of Boston resented the soldiers who had little to do and often spent their days gambling. One officer lost his horse, Sherry, in a card game to a man who owned a glue factory. The new owner treated Sherry so badly that a group of citizens took the horse away and gave it to Paul Revere. Paul had no barn so he housed the horse in a lean-to next to his house and began taking riding lessons. Discover how Sherry becomes a very famous horse, indeed, with her novice rider in <u>Mr. Revere and I</u>.

1. What CAUSED the soldiers to gamble? _____

    _____

2. What was the EFFECT of their gambling?_____

    _____

3. What CAUSED an officer to lose his horse?_____

    _____

4. What was the EFFECT on the horse of being won by a new owner?

    _____

5. What CAUSED the citizens to take the horse away from the new owner?

    _____

6. What was the EFFECT of Paul Revere having a new horse?

    _____

→ Example ←

Grades 5-6   Objectives R2, R3, R4, S5, S6, S10

<u>**The Door in the Wall**</u> by Marguerite deAngeli, Doubleday, 1949.

ACTIVITY Answer the cause and effect questions that follow.

📖 BOOKTALK

In this book of historical fiction, we meet Robin, son of a nobleman and destined to become a knight of the king. However, destiny has a way of playing cruel jokes on one's hopes and dreams, especially when you live during the Middle Ages.

Robin had to be brave when his father left to fight the Scots and when his mother was called away to care for the Queen. He was brave when he became sick and his legs would no longer hold him up or could even be felt. But, when the servants deserted him and he was left alone, he began to doubt how long he could hold on.

Brother Luke saves his life, but Robin must face many problems and dangers. Is his father dead on the battlefield? Will his mother ever return and find him? What is to become of him without the use of his legs? How could he ever serve his king?

All these questions were answered when the castle came under attack, and Robin had to find a way to save it. It was then that Robin found his door in the wall.

1. Because Robin was the son of a nobleman he was (effect)_____

   _____

2. Because Robin's father was off fighting the Scots and his mother had been summoned by the Queen, he was (effect)_____

   _____

3. Because Robin became sick, his legs (effect)_____

   _____

4. Because the servants deserted him Robin (effect)_____

   _____

5. Because Robin lost the use of his legs (effect) _____

   _____

→Example←

Grades 3-4   Objectives R4, S3, S7

ACTIVITY Explore the economic concepts of wants and needs with <u>Charlie and the Chocolate Factory</u> by Roald Dahl. Knopf, 1973.

📖 BOOKTALK

A young boy, about the age of 10, lives with his parents and grandparents in a small house. They don't have very much money and he rarely gets to do exciting things until one very exciting day. He is one of five children to visit a chocolate factory where the world's most wonderful chocolate is made. What happens when he passes through the doors? What happens when one by one the children disappear?

A. What would a single candy bar mean to:

1. A spoiled rich girl who screams until she gets what she wants

_____

2. A starving boy

_____

3. A little man who owns the most famous candy factory in the world

_____

B. What would a four room house mean to:

1. A family who all share one room

_____

2. A wealthy factory owner who lives in a mansion

_____

3. A person who builds homes

_____

C. What would a camera mean to:

1. A ten-year-old boy

_____

_____

2. A bank robber

_____

3. A movie star

_____

→ Example ←

Grades 5-6   Objectives R4, S3, S7

The Haymeadow by Gary Paulsen. Delacorte, 1992.

📖 **BOOKTALK**

At 14 John Barron is asked, like his father and his father's father before him, to spend the summer taking care of their sheep in the haymeadow. *Six thousand sheep.* John will be alone, except for two horses, four dogs, and all those sheep.

John doesn't feel up to the task but he hopes against hope that if he can accomplish it,

he will finally please his undemonstrative father. But John finds that the adage *"things just happen to sheep"* is true when the river floods, coyotes attack, and one dog's feet get cut.

Through it all he relies on his own resourcefulness, ingenuity, and talents to try to get through.

© Nancy Polette

ACTIVITY Write a sentence describing:

1. A bobcat from the point of view of a zoo curator.

_____

2. A bobcat from John's point of view.

_____

3. A sheep ranch from the point of view of the corporation that owns it.

_____

4. A sheep ranch from John's father's point of view.

_____

5. A rattlesnake from the point of view of a herpetologist.

_____

6. A rattlesnake from John's point of view.

_____

7. An injured dog from the point of view of a veterinarian.

_____

8. An injured dog from John' s point of view.

_____

9. A sheep stampede from the point of view of a person watching it on television.

_____

10. A sheep stampede from John's point of view.

_____

→Example←

Grades 3-4   Objectives R6, R8, R9

Good tunes for summarizing are *Skip To My Lou* and *My Bonnie Lies Over the Ocean*. Words can be left out for classmates to add using a modified cloze procedure.

Charlotte's Web by E. B. White. HarperCollins, 1952.

📖 BOOKTALK

Wilbur, the pig, is sold to Fern's Uncle who decides to fatten him up for the butcher, but Wilbur's friend, Charlotte, the spider, finds a way to save him by spinning messages about him in her web. Wilbur truly becomes the prize pig at the fair!

ACTIVITY A Song About Charlotte After hearing the booktalk, how many words can you complete in this song? Sing the song to the tune of *My Bonnie Lies Over the Ocean*.

Verse
Oh, this is a song about (1) C _____
A (2) s _____ so gentle and good,
Who promised a small (3) p _____ named (4) W _____
She'd save him if anyone could.
 Chorus
 (5) W _____ , (6) C _____
 And (7) T _____ lived on a tidy farm
 (8) C _____ promised
 To rescue poor (9) W _____ from harm.
  Verse
  Now (10) F _____ sold uncle the piglet
  He then tried to (11) f _____ the beast
  To take a plump pig to the (12) b _____
  And turn him into a ham (13) f _____ .
   Verse
   So (14) C _____ spins a wordy message
   To tell the world about her friend,
   And (15) W _____ is saved from the butcher
   To bring this fine tale to an (16) e _____ .

→Example←

Grades 3-4   Objectives R6, R8, R9

Young Nick and Jubilee by Leon Garfield. Delacorte Press, 1989.

📖 BOOKTALK

Nick and his sister are orphans trying to survive on the London streets. They steal food and hide out in the park at night. Nick worries that he will never get enough money for a dowry for his sister and thus will never be rid of her. Then he hears a man offer 50 pounds reward for a stolen watch. Nick is determined to find the watch even though the places he must look are the most dangerous in all London.

A London Rap

ACTIVITY Enjoy doing this rap in your class. Assign various parts to different individuals or groups. If you have read the book, add more rap verses.

Once in London Town oh so very long ago,
Nick hurried and he scurried in the gaslight's glow,
To a creepy, crawly cave in St. James Park,
Nick and sister Jubilee hid out in the dark.

CHORUS: (repeat)

Bluebottles coming
With their poking and their peering lights,
Bluebottles coming
Giving little children frights.

Now Jubilee was hungry, there was nothing to eat,
So Nick turned to stealing on a London street.
Black holes between the houses, rubbish heaps piled high,
Twiggy shadows like arms stretched from ground to sky.

CHORUS: (repeat)

Bluebottles coming
With their poking and their peering lights,
Bluebottles coming
Giving little children frights.   *(Continued on next page)*

People hurried by on the London street,
Starving children's eyes they refused to meet.
Raddish-faced girls, stuck out chins, twisted ears,
They ignored the little ones and their hungry tears.

CHORUS: (repeat)

Bluebottles coming
With their poking and their peering lights,
Bluebottles coming
Giving little children frights.

Once in your hometown oh not very long ago
There were people without homes and their lives were filled with woe.
Did the people in your town with their eyes and their ears,
Ignore the homeless folk and their hungry tears?

CHORUS: (repeat)

Bluebottles coming
Seeking homeless folk to offer aid.
Bluebottles coming
On a mercy raid!

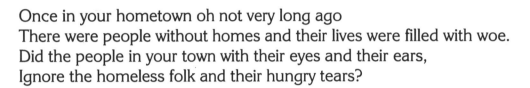

Strategy Twenty-three: Storyboards

→ Example ←

Grades 3-6   Objectives R2, R5, R6, R9, S10

ACTIVITY Writing a Sequel to a Story

1. The storyboard on the next page has ten spaces. Space one is the character/setting space. In this space write the names of two characters from the story or novel you have read. Place the characters in a new setting. Write the name of the setting in this space as well.

What time of day is it? What time of year is it?

2. Cut apart the incident cards. These are the incidents that move the story along. Choose one you think will fit in space two.

3. Space three is the problem. This means conflict. What does one character want to do or where does one character want to go that the other does not?

4. Space eight is the climax point of your story. The most exciting part of the story should happen here.

5. Continue moving the story along by placing incident cards in the empty spaces. By the time you reach space 10 you should have solved the problem presented in space three.

Storyboards

Fill the blank spaces on the storyboard below with the incident cards. Be sure in developing the story that the problem (space 3) and solution (space 10) match!

Storyboard

1. Character/ Setting	6.
2.	7.
3. Problem	8. Climax
4.	9.
5.	10. Solution

Incident Cards

A bargain is made	It rains	Someone walks away
Someone runs	An army approaches	There's a knock at the door
An invitation arrives	The order is given	An animal escapes
A bottle is found	The cloud covers the sun	A magic ring is found
The earth trembles	There is silence	The load was heavy
They travel together	The sun comes up	Someone smiles
Someone sings	It is caught	Someone screams
Footsteps are heard	A bird appears	The search begins
The fight begins	The noise gets louder	They can't find it
It is invisible	It drops	It is fixed

When the storyboard is completed you are ready to write your own story.

Strategy Twenty-four: Responding With Visuals

After analyzing the text the student will demonstrate understanding by drawing or adding to a drawing to emphasize a particular point.

→ Example ←

Grades 3-4   Objectives R2, R3, R4, R6, S3

Beezus and Ramona by Beverly Cleary. Morrow, 1955.

📖 BOOKTALK

Having a little sister can be great! But having a little sister like Ramona can be just plain exasperating! Nine-year-old Beezus tries very hard to do the right things and make the best of her time, but four-year-old Ramona keeps getting in the way and ruining things for Beezus.

Beezus wants so much to love her sister like her mother and Aunt Beatrice love each other. Beezus finds it very difficult to love a sister who's always doing annoying things, like jumping around wearing paper bunny ears in public and yelling *"read Scoopy."*

Read this wonderfully hilarious book about sisters to see how Beezus handles her relationship with silly Ramona.

ACTIVITY Suppose these children showed up at Ramona's party to discover there was no party. Draw expressions on their faces to show how each might feel.

© Nancy Polette

<u>Grades 5-6</u>   <u>Objectives R2, R3, R4, R6, S3</u>

<u>**Mrs. Frisby and the Rats of NIMH**</u> by Robert C. O'Brien. Harper-Collins, 1986.

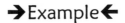 **BOOKTALK**

The Frisbys are a mouse family that live in Mr. Fitzgibbon's garden. Each spring they move from their cinderblock house in the garden to the field where they're safe from his plow. Late in the winter the Frisbys are faced with a shortage of food. Timothy (the youngest boy) has come down with pneumonia, and Mr. Fitzgibbon is warming up his plow. Mrs. Frisby, being a widow, has to face all of these hardships with her children. Jeremy, a kindhearted crow, takes her to the owl for advice. The owl sends her to the mysteriously intelligent rats for help.

ACTIVITY

The rats found a tinker's toy and put many of them to use in creating their new civilization. Suppose that the Skinner Enterprise truck below was that of the toy tinker. What item might have fallen out of the truck? (Add one to the picture). How could it be used by the rats in their new civilization? Show as a drawing.

Strategy Twenty-five: Writing Dialogue

Partners pretend they are onlookers to an incident in a story or novel. They write and perform a dialogue telling what they saw.

→ Example ←

Grades 3-4   Objectives R3, R4, R8, R9, S3, S9

Homer Price by Robert McCloskey. Viking, 1943.

📖 BOOKTALK

Homer Price was working in Uncle Ulysses's lunch room one day when an automatic doughnut machine could not be stopped. Uncle Ulysses was playing pinochle at the local barbershop and didn't get back to help Homer shut off the machine. Homer wasn't able to solve the problem. Mr. Gabby, a sandwich man, tried to help, but he and Homer decided they'd just have to wait until the batter ran out. With so many doughnuts, Homer realized that Mr. Gabby might advertise them on the sandwich boards he wore while walking up and down the street.

However, the doughnuts did not start selling before another problem popped up. Miss Enders and her chauffeur returned when they discovered she had lost her diamond bracelet while mixing her favorite doughnut recipe for the lunch room earlier that day. It dawned on Homer that the lost bracelet must be in one of the doughnuts. Mr. Gabby made a new sign telling of the $100 prize for the one who found the bracelet. When all but a few hundred doughnuts had been eaten, Rupert Black bit into the lucky doughnut and was declared the winner. Mr. Gabby called it one of the best tricks of merchandising he had ever seen and everyone went home happy.

ACTIVITY Write a dialogue between two lunch room customers who have come in to eat doughnuts, hoping to win the $100.00 prize. Think about . . .

A. Who else would they see in the lunch room?

B. What would the doughnut machine be doing?

C. What would they do with the $100.00 if they won it?

D. The importance of advertising in selling goods and services.

Grades 5-6   Objectives R3, R4, R8, R9, S3, S9

The Pushcart War by Jean Merrill. HarperCollins, 1964.

📖 BOOKTALK

The Pushcart War started on the afternoon of March 15, 1976, when a truck ran down a pushcart belonging to a flower peddler. The pushcart was flattened and the owner of the pushcart was pitched head first into a pickle barrel.

This was only the first incident in a war that lasted four months in the traffic-snarled streets of New York. The trucks had become so aggressive and reckless that the pushcart peddlers had no choice but to fight back. Under the leadership of Maxie Hammerman, the Pushcart King, they developed a strategy to outwit the truckers and the corrupt politicians who backed them.

The use of a secret weapon, a modified pea shooter, was crucial to the strategy. Finally, when a movie star, the children of New York and the general public got involved, the truckers were in more trouble than ever expected.

ACTIVITY Write a dialogue between two pushcart peddlers who have gathered at Maxie Hammerman's shop to discuss what to do about the attacks by the big trucks.

Include as many of these economic terms as you can in the dialogue.

A. risk capital

B. monopoly

C. price war

D. consignment

E. mass production

F. investment in human resources

G. incentive/reward system

H. opportunity cost

I. advertising

J. diversification

K. risk

Strategy Twenty-six: Analyzing Characters

Choose a character from a story or novel. List four characteristics of the character. Under each characteristic give at least three pieces of evidence to support the trait.

→ Example ←

Grades 3-4   Objectives R2, R3, S7, S9

__Stone Fox__ by John Gardiner. HarperCollins, 1980.

📖 BOOKTALK

Little Willy was worried. Not just a little bit worried like when he overslept that one morning and found the chickens had eaten his breakfast, but a lot worried. The worry began the morning Grandfather would not get out of bed. Grandfather was usually the first one up and had half the farm chores done before Willy stirred. On the morning Grandfather did not get up, Willy was so worried that he ran to get the doctor. She gave Grandfather a real thorough examination but could find nothing wrong with him. *"Some folks just decide to stop living,"* she said, *"and there is not much anyone can do about it until they change their minds."*

Willy was determined to get Grandfather to change his mind! The potato crop was ready for harvest and Willy managed it alone by hitching up his dog, Searchlight, to the plow. But when the tax man came Willy didn't know what to do.

The tax man talked about selling the farm for back taxes. *"But we always pay the bills on time,"* Willy protested. *"Not the tax bills,"* the tax man replied. *"You owe ten years back taxes. That comes to about five hundred dollars."*

Five hundred dollars! Willy had never seen so much money. Grandfather couldn't help. He just laid in bed and stared at the ceiling. How was Willy going to raise five hundred dollars? He watched the taxman's retreating back. *"You can't take our farm!"* Willy screamed.

The tax man turned around and smiled through his yellow-stained teeth. *"Oh, yes we can,"* he said.

ACTIVITY From the booktalk list three characteristics of Willy and at least one piece of evidence to support each.

Characteristic_____   Evidence _____

Characteristic_____   Evidence _____

Characteristic_____   Evidence _____

→ Example ←

Johnny Tremain by Esther Forbes. Houghton-Mifflin, 1943.

📖 BOOKTALK

Clever and gifted Johnny Tremain is apprenticed to a silversmith in the year 1773. Johnny sees a great future ahead until the day that carelessness caused his hand to be so badly burned that his dreams of being a silversmith were gone. Johnny becomes bitter and feels useless until he becomes a dispatch rider for the Committee of Public Safety and gets to know the leaders of the Revolution. With the rapid events that follow leading to independence, Johnny fills a valuable role in securing the nation's freedom from English oppression. Live through two years of history with Johnny Tremain and watch through his eyes as the revolution unfolds.

ACTIVITY From the booktalk list four characteristics that apply to Johnny.

Give at least one piece of evidence to support each character trait you list.

Characteristic_____   Evidence_____

_____   _____

Characteristic_____   Evidence_____

_____   _____

Characteristic_____   Evidence_____

_____   _____

Characteristic_____   Evidence_____

_____   _____

→ Example ←

Grades 3-4   Objectives R4, R8, S10

The Chocolate Touch by Patrick Skene Catling. Morrow, 1952.

📖 BOOKTALK

This funny, moral tale about a greedy boy's comeuppance has been beloved by children since its first appearance in 1952. Inspired by the legend of the avaricious king whose touch turned all to gold, Mr. Catling conceived a modern variation that delights as it instructs. In it a boy's lust for chocolate becomes the fatal flaw.

The story tells of two days after John acquired the chocolate touch, the magic that turned everything his lips touched into chocolate. At first, John was elated with his discovery. Now at last he could have all the chocolate he wanted. Chocolate toothpaste was delicious; chocolate bacon and chocolate eggs were even better. But soon he began to get awfully thirsty, and before the day was over John suspected that his sweet dream-come-true might have its bitter side.

ACTIVITY

Debate

Reasons the Chocolate Touch **would be** good to have:	Reasons the Chocolate Touch **would not** be good to have:

© Nancy Polette

Grades 5-6   Objectives R4, R8, S10

Beyond the Western Sea: Book One by Avi. Orchard, 1996.

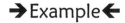 📖 **BOOKTALK**

The people of a small Irish village watch in despair as their homes are destroyed on orders of the overseer. Patrick, Maura and Mother are luckier than most since they have tickets to America that father sent so that they can join him there.

Patrick throws a stone, hitting the overseer, and is threatened with deportation to a prison colony. He runs away and Maura and Mother are breathless when they finally catch up with him.

The three reach the city of Cork and arrive at the docks just as the boarding call is being given for the ship they are to take. But Mother refuses to board the ship. She insists that she will go back to her home in the village even though there is no home to go back to. Maura pleads with her to board the ship but she refuses. What should Maura do?

ACTIVITY

Debate

Give reasons why Maura should **stay** with her mother	Give reasons why Maura should **get on the ship**

Strategy Twenty-eight: The Data Bank

The Data Bank is a way to stop copying by organizing information under predetermined headings given to students by the teacher. The student gathers three or more facts under each heading.

→ Example ←

Grades 3-4   Objectives R5, R6, R9, S2, S7

Headings for an animal report could be:

Where it lives   _What it eats_   _What it does_   _What it has_   _What it looks like_

Kilroy and the Gull by Nathaniel Benchley. HarperCollins, 1977.

📖 BOOKTALK

Kilroy is a normal young member of a pod of killer whales until humans capture him and put him into a Marineland aquarium. Then Kilroy proves that he is a very special sort: first, because he likes to do tricks for fun, not fish; and second, because he makes friends with Morris the seagull.

With Morris's help, Kilroy is able to trick the humans and rejoin his pod in the open sea. But Kilroy is different now. He is curious about humans. Somehow he feels that it is possible to communicate with them, and he is determined to find a way.

ACTIVITY Add more information under each heading.

A Whale Data Bank

LIVES
ocean
cold water
warm water

_____
_____

EATS
fish
plankton
shrimp

_____
_____

HAS
blubber
flippers
bumpy skin

_____
_____

DOES
breathes air
does tricks

_____
_____

LOOKS LIKE
mountain in the sea
huge sea lion

_____
_____

Grades 5-6   Objectives R5, R6, R9, S2, S7

Headings for People

Description   *Related To*   *Accomplishments*

Lived   *Talents*   *Fears*

Headings for Places

Location   *Climate*   *Land Forms*

Products   *Plants*   *Animals*   *Historical Events*

Headings for non-living Objects

Description   *Uses*   *Made Of*

Where Found   *Unique Features*

Susanna of the Alamo by John Jakes. Harcourt, 1986.

📖 BOOKTALK

"Remember the Alamo!" is a cry that evokes memories of Davy Crockett, Jim Bowie, and William Barrett Travis . . . three of the many heroes who died there. But few remember Susanna Dickinson, the woman of quiet courage and unwavering resolve who survived the massacre to tell its story. Were it not for Susanna, the Alamo might have been forgotten.

Susanna was spared death at the Alamo by Mexico's General Santa Anna so that she could bear witness of his might to Sam Houston's rebel Texas army. But Susanna scorned the general's attempt to make her his emissary. Her chilling story instead provoked a rage and inspired a memory that fired the strength of Houston's badly outnumbered Texans. They decisively defeated Santa Anna at San Jacinto and this victory assured Texas's independence from Mexico.

LOCATION	DESCRIPTION	PURPOSE
Texas	High walls	Spanish mission
In San Antonio	Small	Used as fort

EVENTS	PEOPLE INVOLVED	OTHER FACTS
Battle 1836	Lt. Col. William Travis	Important to Texas' independence
Texas vs Mexico	Jim Bowie	Gave Sam Houston time to build an
All Texans killed	Davy Crockett	army
except women	Santa Anna	
and children		

Excellent sources of information are The Alamo by Leonard Everett Fisher. Holiday House, 1987; and The Alamo by Herman Silverstein. Dillon Press, 1992.

Using The Data Bank Information

There are many ways to share the information in the data bank with others. On the pages that follow are patterns you can use in organizing and sharing this information in creative ways.

The Only One Pattern

Study this pattern. What other items of information from the data bank can you add, using the pattern?

ONLY ONE ALAMO

San Antonio has many buildings
But ONLY ONE ALAMO!
In 1836 the Alamo was attacked by 4000 men
In ONLY ONE ARMY

_____

_____

_____

_____

_____

Grades 5-6   Objectives R5, R6, R9 S2, S7

Kate Shelley: Bound for Legend by Robert D. SanSouci. Dial Books, 1995.

📖 BOOKTALK

Once in a while an ordinary person performs a deed so brave and unexpected that we remember it long afterward. Kate Shelley was such a person. In the midst of a torrential storm in the summer of 1881, a dreadful train wreck occurred near fifteen-year-old Kate's Iowa farm. Instantly Kate knew she must go for help and warn an oncoming train of the danger up ahead. Risking her life, she set out through the treacherous night to find the survivors of the wreck, then crawled over the slippery tracks of a 700 foot railroad bridge on her rescue mission. This is the tale of an unforgettable young girl whose great courage and humanity are still remembered today.

Kate Shelley Data Bank

Lived	*Description*	*Had*	*What She Did*
Iowa - 1881	15 years old	little schooling	plowed and planted
near Honey Creek	dark hair	love of railroads	ran the family farm
by train tracks	work-worn hands	determination	shot hawks
on a farm	courageous	sense of duty	rode bareback
near a river	responsible	inner strength	read a lot
clapboard house	hard working	a bridge named after her	prevented a train wreck
			saved lives of two men
			made a dangerous journey alone

Related To
deceased father (railroad man)
invalid mother
sister Mayme, brother John
deceased brother James

Remembered For
Making a dangerous journey alone at night in a storm to stop trains from crossing a bridge that was out.

→Example←

Grades 3-6   Objectives R5, R6, R9, S1, S9, S10

A. Patterns for Reporting about Animals

If I Were **Pattern**

a. Name the thing you want to be.   _____

b. Where is it found?   _____

c. One thing it would do for someone else.   _____

d. A second thing it would do.   _____

e. Repeat the first line.   _____

Example:

If I were a lobster

Snug in my hole in the ocean floor,

I would crawl out and tell you good morning

And wave my claws at you,

If I were a lobster.

© Nancy Polette   CLC0223 Pieces of Learning

Your Turn

If I were a _____

_____

I would _____

And _____

If I were a _____

The Chant

(From a data bank choose six facts for the first verse and seven facts for the second
 verse.)

An Alligator Chant

Facts about alligators:

Eats fish	Strong legs
And snakes	Lays eggs
Thick body	Lives 60 years
Sharp teeth	Dull gray
Tough skin	18 ft
Like a lizard	500 lbs
These are just a few	Nest of grass, too.
	From near and far
	Here they are
	Facts about alligators!

**The Important Thing About**

The Important Book by Margaret Wise Brown. Harper,1993.

The important thing about _____ IS _____
    (Add six to eight details)
    (Repeat the first sentence.)

Example

The important thing about **a whale** is that **it always knows where it is in the ocean.** It eats fish and plankton and shrimp. It has flippers and a blowhole. It swims in the ocean in both warm and cold water. It breathes air and does tricks. But **the important thing about a whale is that it always knows where it is in the ocean.**

**Compare/contrast Pattern**

    If I had the _____ of a _____

    I would _____

And I'd _____

And _____

But I wouldn't _____

Because _____ s do that.

B. Patterns for Reporting about People

**Bio Poem**

First name _____   Who needs _____

Four traits_____ _____   Who gives _____

_____ _____   Who fears _____

Related to _____   Who would like to see _____

Cares deeply about _____   Resident of _____

Who feels _____

     © Nancy Polette   CLC0223 Pieces of Learning

Acrostic

W ar correspondent

I n South Africa, 1899

N otorious Boer enemy

S eizes armored

T rain

O f those aboard, he is captured

N o hope of escape.

C hecks out prison camp.

H igh walls, floodlights, sentries.

U p, over the wall, in an unguarded moment.

R acing heart, he scales the heights,

C amp left behind.

H opping railroad cars

I n dead of night finds British help.

L auded as a hero.

L eader of the future.

Fortunately/Unfortunately

Fortunately John Hancock lived next door to a wishing stone.
Unfortunately he never got what he wished for.
Fortunately he was very wealthy.
Unfortunately he could not buy friendship.

What Ever Happened to

What ever happened to _____

Did she _____

Maybe she _____

Or could it be that _____

Was there _____

Maybe someday we will know the truth that _____

Why report

Choose one incident in the life of a person. In one-half page explain WHY
it happened.

Example   Why did Kate save the train?
Why was George Washington the first President of the United
States?

C. Patterns for Reporting about Places and Events

Write a Song (Tune: This Land Is Your Land)

As I was walking through (name a city, state, province or country)

I saw _____ and _____

I saw _____ and the _____

Interesting sights for all to see. (Add more verses)

© Nancy Polette   CLC0223 Pieces of Learning

<u>Geography Riddle Report</u>

Copy the first line. List 6-8 sights one would see. Copy the line, *"But that's not all."* List six to eight more sights. Finally, ask, *"Where am I?"*

Example

Let's go to long ago places and see the earth's changing faces.
We will see . . .
Spaniards creeping through a city toward a lake
Tlaxcalan allies at their sides
Reaching the eastern causeway to the mainland
Moving silently
Seen by women fetching water from the lake

But that's not all.

600 men heading for only one bridge
Warriors in pursuit
Letting loose a deadly hail of stones
Spaniards drowning in heavy armor
Murderous invaders lying dead by the thousands
Still clinging greedily to their stolen gold.

WHERE AM I?   *June 30, 1520*
                 The Spanish disaster at the capital city
                 of the Aztec Empire.

<u>Fact and Fiction Book</u>

Make a statement about the characters, events, or setting on one page. On the next page tell your reader whether the statement is fact or fiction and why.

→ Example ←

Grades 3-6   Objectives R3, R4, R5, S10

George Washington's Socks by Elvira Woodruff. Scholastic, 1996.

📖 BOOKTALK

Matthew was president of the Adventure Club and planning the first all night camp-out in Tony's backyard when disaster struck. Matthew couldn't go unless little sister Katie went along! So that night, the boys, with Katie tagging along, decide to take a walk along the river bank and find an old row boat. This is too good a chance to pass up, Matthew thinks, as the children climb into the boat. Before long the children are lost in a velvety darkness, moved along by a strong current in a river choked with ice. And then it happened. The boat tipped and Katie went overboard. After a frantic search, another boat appears. In the center stands George Washington holding a wet and sleeping Katie in his arms. *"Arrest the Tory spies,"* the General calls out, pointing to Matt's boat. The boys were speechless. Was this some TV show gag, or had they somehow gone back in time?

ACTIVITY Thinking about the colonies and the American Revolution . . .

Fluency The ability to make many responses

How many words can you think of to describe George Washington?

Flexibility The ability to respond in a variety of areas

A. Into how many groups can you put your list of words?

B. Select two famous people from American history. List as many ways as you can that these two people are alike.

Originality Responding in new or unique ways

Suppose a new boy suddenly appears in your neighborhood. He looks like all your other friends, but you suspect he has been transported from another period of history. What behavior would give him away? How could you discover what period he was from?

**Analogy**   A comparison which points out similarities between two things that might be different in other respects.

Examples

A. George Washington is to the Revolutionary War as Abraham Lincoln is to the Civil War.

B. Betsy Ross is to flag as Francis Scott Key is to anthem.

Complete these!

A. Thomas Jefferson is to Monticello as George Washington is to _____ .

B. Benjamin Franklin is to printing as Paul Revere is to _____ .

**Associative Thinking**   Similar to analogy in which we find a common area among two or more seemingly dissimilar persons, places, events or objects.

Example A ship is just a ship until it is the scene of the Boston Tea Party. Then it becomes a symbol of revolution.

Complete these . . .

A. Valley Forge was just a place until _____

_____and then it became _____

B. Paul Revere's horse was just a horse until_____

_____and then it became_____

C. A writing pen was just a writing pen until _____

_____and then it became_____

D. The Thirteen Colonies were just thirteen colonies until_____

_____and then they became_____

Attribute Listing   Observing and identifying qualities of a particular object.

ACTIVITY   List the attributes (qualities) of a leader.

_____   _____
_____   _____
_____   _____

Choose a famous leader and use the attributes you listed in a poem.

Follow this pattern:

Line One: Name _____

Line Two: Two attributes _____   _____

Line Three: Three things the person does (use _ing_ words)

_____   _____   _____

Line Four: Four words that show feeling _____   _____

_____   _____

Line Five: Synonym for line one   _____

Evaluation   Listing desirable and undesirable aspects of an object or situation.

ACTIVITY   List the positive and negative aspects of not going to school.

Positive	Negative

© Nancy Polette   CLC0223 Pieces of Learning

Generalization   Forming a rule that explains a number of given situations.

Step One Collect, organize, and examine the material.

For example, examine this list of books by Jean Fritz.

And Then What Happened, Paul Revere?
Bully for You, Teddy Roosevelt
Can't You Make Them Behave, King George?
Double Life of Pocahontas
George Washington's Breakfast

Step Two Identify what these titles have in common.

_____

_____

Step Three Make a general statement about books written by Jean Fritz.

In general, books by Jean Fritz are _____

_____

Step Four Find other books by Jean Fritz to see if this generalization can be supported with additional evidence.

Planning

1. Determine what is to be done.

_____

2. Determine needed materials.

_____

3. List steps in order.

_____

4. Predict problems.

_____

5. Determine possibility of success.

_____

ACTIVITY Plan how you would show the many problems faced by Washington's army at Valley Forge.

A. How will you discover what the problems were?

B. What will be the best means of sharing this information with others?

C. What materials will you need?

D. What will you do first, second, last?

E. What problems might you have in finding information or in locating and organizing materials?

**Sequencing**   To order events or items according to ascending or descending size or value

ACTIVITY Place the events listed below in order to answer the questions:

1. Was King Tut murdered? If so, who was the murderer?

2. How many times and who did Ay marry?

_____ Birth Announcement: Mr. & Mrs. Ay are proud new grandparents of a baby girl named Ankhesenamum (Ank for short).

_____ Uncle Ay's Journal Entry: Tut will never guess the enormous power I now have!

_____ News Headline: Nine-year-old King Tut assumes throne. Uncle to act as advisor.

_____ News Headline: Mysterious Death of 18-year-old Tut.

_____ Marriage Announcement: 17-year-old Tut marries Ankhesenamum and makes her his queen.

_____ Conversation between Tut and Wife: It is time I began to rule Egypt. Uncle Ay must go.

_____ Death Notice: Mrs. Ay dies.

_____ Marriage Announcement: Ay, advisor to deceased King Tut, marries King's widow and becomes the new King.

Strategy Thirty-one: Pick A Project Chart

This chart allows choice of topic, verb and product and enables the student to make a clear task statement in responding either to fiction or non fiction.

➜ Example ⬅

Grades 3-4   Objectives R5, R6, R9, S9

Strawberry Girl by Lois Lenski. Lippincott, 1945.

📖 BOOKTALK

When her family moves into the old Roddenberry place, ten-year-old Birdie Boyer looks forward to happy times. Her father says they'll raise sugar cane, oranges and even a crop of strawberries and Birdie can't wait to be a strawberry girl. But after their new neighbors, the Slaters, pay them a visit, Birdie senses trouble ahead. It's not easy fighting the heat, drought, and cold spells to raise Florida strawberries. When your neighbors are determined to start a feud, is it impossible?

ACTIVITY

Step One (Choose and circle one action word)	Step Two (Choose and circle one topic)	Step Three (Choose and circle one product)
Label	**Literature Response Projects** The theme of hard work in the story The setting of the story as it affects the plot	Acrostic poem
List	The change in Mr. Slater from the beginning to the end of the story - causes and effects	Chart
Describe	Mr. Boyer's attitude toward animals The characters of Birdie and Shoestring How they are alike and different	Dictionary
Locate		Story
Report	Conflict in the story: between the Slaters and the Boyers; between nature and people	Model
Show	**Research Projects** Florida: wild creatures and plants of the swamplands	Map Mobile
Compare	Underground lakes, sinkholes, bogs Grasshopper swarms; effect on crops Making paper flowers	Diorama
Discover	Designing hats From sugar cane to sugar The Big Freeze of 1895	Bio-poem
Compose	Products from strawberries	Pattern Report

Grades 5-6   Objectives R5, R6, R9, S9

The Wolves of Willoughby Chase by Joan Aiken. Doubleday, 1962.

📖 BOOKTALK

Wicked wolves without and a grim governess within the great English country house of Willoughby Chase prove sore trials to brave and determined Bonnie, her cousin Sylvia, and their faithful friend Simon.

Little did the girls dream, when Bonnie's parents left them in the care of the terrible Miss Slighcarp, what the future would hold. Their life at the Chase seemed almost unendurable but then Miss Slighcarp sent them off to her sister, brutal Mrs. Brisket, and her daughter, the awful Diana. With only Simon to help them, Bonnie and Sylvia face many chilly moments in this tale of adventure and suspense.

ACTIVITY

Action (Choose one)	Topic (Choose One) Non-Fiction	Product (Choose One)
Knowledge		Acrostic poem
Define		Advice letter
Record	Trains 100 years ago and	Autobiography
Label	trains today	Bio-poem
List	Why there are fewer passenger	Chart
	trains in the world today than ever	Comic strip
Comprehension	before	Diorama
Summarize	The effect of winter on wildlife in	Editorial
Describe	the forest	Essay
Locate	Things needed for life in a cave	Eyewitness report
Report	Unusual books about train travel	Interview
	Wildlife found in a typical forest	Journal
Application	London 100 years ago and today	Moment in history script
Solve	Unusual words in the story and	Mystery person report
Demonstrate	their meaning	Newspaper
Dramatize	Statements made about wolves in	Oral report
Show	the story	Poem
	Effects of winter on rivers	Question/answer session
Synthesis		Readers theatre script
Compose	**Literature Response Topics**	Report
Hypothesize		Song
Predict		Story
Create	Ways in which this story is like	Tape recording
	Snow White	Time line
Evaluation	The characters of the 2 girls	TV script
Judge	The theme of good versus evil	True/false book
Rank Order	Simon's role in the story	

© Nancy Polette

SIDEWAYS STORIES FROM WAYSIDE SCHOOL

A NOVEL UNIT

WITH EMPHASIS ON

THINKING SKILLS

ABOUT THE BOOK

There had been a terrible mistake. Wayside School was supposed to be built with thirty classrooms all next to each other in a row. Instead, they built the classrooms one on top of the other...thirty stories tall! The builder said he was terribly sorry.

That may be why all kinds of funny things happen at Wayside School, especially on the thirtieth floor. You'll meet Mrs. Gorf, the meanest teacher of all, terrible Todd, who always gets sent home early and John, who can read only upside down. This is a school where children are turned into apples, dead rats wear raincoats, mosquito bites are turned into numbers, names are traded and walls laugh. It's a crazy mixed-up school sure to bring laughs that come out-sideways!

ABOUT THE AUTHOR

Louis Sachar lives in Austin, Texas, with his wife, Carla, their daughter, Sherre, and the family dog, Lucky. He trained as a lawyer and plays chess and rugby in addition to writing many popular children's books including Someday Angeline, Johnny's in the Basement and the hilarious Marvin Redpost series, all published by Avon.

ABOUT THE ACTIVITIES

Each activity page is designed to teach a particular thinking skill. Students will respond to the stories both orally and in writing using fourteen different skills - analogy, analysis, attribute listing, decision making, elaboration, evaluation, fluency, flexible thinking, generalization, listing, planning, sequencing, forecasting, and webbing.

ANALOGY

A comparison which points out similarities between two things that might be different in other respects.

Chapter 1. *Mrs. Gorf* was such a mean teacher, if you displeased her she would turn you into an apple.

Chapter 2. *Mrs. Jewls,* the nice new teacher, thinks her students are monkeys.

ACTIVITY

Study the Examples

Shoe is to **foot** as mitten is to **hand**.
Scissors is to **hair** as lawn mower is to **grass**.
Mother is to **woman** as father is to **man**.
Fish is to **swim** as bird is to **fly**.

Complete these *Wayside School* analogies.

A. Custodian is to furnace room as principal is to _____
B. Children are to school as nurses are to _____
C. Tongue is to mouth as brain is to _____
D. Wiggle is to ears as sniff is to _____
E. Apple is to tree as corn is to _____
F. Sun is to day as _____ is to night.
G. Tears are to crying as _____ are to laughing.
H. Louis is to yard as Mrs. Gorf is to _____
I. Tomato is to spaghetti sauce as apple is to _____
J. Mrs. Jewls is to nice as the Wicked Witch of the West is to _____
K. Pig is to pen as monkey is to _____
L. Lettuce is to rabbits as peanuts are to _____
M. Song is to sing as _____ is to read.

Answers

(A) office (B) hospital (C) head (D) nose (E) stalk (F) moon (G) smiles (H) classroom (I) applesauce (J) mean (K) tree

(L) elephants (M) book (or story)

Chapter 3. *Joe* couldn't count even though he came up with the right answers.

Chapter 4. *Sharie* didn't wake up until she had fallen 10 stories out the window.

ANALYZE

	ALIKE	**DIFFERENT**
Characters (Joe and Sharie)		
Story Settings		
Plot of the Stories		
Mood of the stories		
Lessons the stories teach		

ATTRIBUTE LISTING

Observing and identifying qualities of a particular object.

Chapter 5. *Todd* can't help getting into trouble for talking.

Chapter 6. *Bebe* can draw 378 pictures in an hour.

ACTIVITY

A. List all the attributes (qualities) of a verbal person.

1. What he or she likes. _____

2. What he or she does. _____

B. List the attributes of an artist.

1. What he or she likes._____

2. What he or she does. _____

Choose either Todd (the talker) or (the artist). Use the attributes you listed in a poem.
Follow this pattern:

Line One Name _____

Line Two Two attributes _____ _____

Line Three Three things the person does (use *ing* words)

_____ _____ _____

Line Four Four words that show feeling

_____   _____

_____   _____

Line Five Synonym for line one _____

DECISION MAKING

Identify the problem. List possible solutions.
Judge solutions with specific criteria.

Chapter 7. *Calvin* is supposed to take a note he doesn't have to a teacher who doesn't exist in a story that was never built. His teacher will be angry if he doesn't do it.

Chapter 8. *Myron* has to decide on what the most important job of a class president is.

ACTIVITY

Help Calvin and Myron make their decisions by working the decision grids that follow. Score 3 if the answer is *yes*, 2 if *maybe* and 1 if *no*. Add the scores for each alternative to see what the best decision will be.

Criteria

ALTERNATIVES The most important job of a class president is . . .	Will it help the class?	Does it need to be done?	Can he do it?	Is it an important job?	Total
1. Listening	2	2	3	2	9
2. Turning on lights					
3. Helping a friend					
4. Your idea					

Criteria

ALTERNATIVES What should Calvin do?	Can he do it?	Will it make his teacher happy?	Is it safe?	Is it low cost?	Total
1. Your idea					
2. Your idea					
3. Your idea					
4. Your idea					

ELABORATION

Adding details to a basic product.

Chapter 9. *Maurecia* had ice cream every day until she got tired of it. Then she didn't like anything or anybody.

Chapter 10. *Paul* gave in to temptation and pulled Leslie's pigtails one at a time.

ACTIVITY

A. Draw an ice cream cone. What could you *add to* it so Maurecia would want to taste it?

B. Draw Leslie's pig tails. What could you *add to* them so that Paul would stop pulling them?

© Nancy Polette

EVALUATION

Listing desirable and undesirable aspects of an object or situation.

Chapter 11. *Dana* turns her mosquito bites into numbers to stop the itching.

Chapter 12. *Jason* sits on a big wad of gum and gets stuck in his chair.

ACTIVITY

Which is the best story? Dana? Or Jason?

Give reasons *Dana* is the best story.	Give reasons *Jason* is the best story.
1. _____	1. _____
2. _____	2. _____
3. _____	3. _____
4. _____	4. _____
5. _____	5. _____
6. _____	6. _____
7. _____	7. _____
8. _____	8. _____
9. _____	9. _____
10. _____	10. _____

The best story is the one with the most reasons given.

The best story is _____

Chapter 13. *Rondi* The class tells Rondi her missing front teeth are cute, the hat she isn't wearing is interesting, and the joke she didn't tell was funny.

Chapter 14. *Sammy*, the new student, gets smaller and smaller as the teacher removes his many raincoats. When the last raincoat comes off all that is left is a dead rat.

ACTIVITY

1. Name all the pieces of clothing that Rondi might not be wearing.

_____

_____

_____

2. Name all the two-inch-high things that might have been under the raincoat instead of a dead rat.

_____

_____

_____

3. Name many other ways Mrs. Jewls might discipline students rather than sending them home on the kindergarten bus.

_____

_____

_____

_____

FLEXIBLE THINKING

Stretching the mind beyond the expected response.

Chapter 15. *Deedee* never gets a good playground ball because she is late getting out to recess.

Chapter 16. *D. J.'s* smile is catching!

ACTIVITY

A. Help Deedee get out to recess early. List as many things as you can that she can do to be allowed to leave the room. Circle your most unusual reason . . . the one you believe no one else will think of.

B. How many kinds of smiles can you name? How can you group your list of smiles?

Kinds of Smiles

_____

_____

_____

_____

_____

_____

_____

_____

Group

S _____
M _____
I _____
L _____
E _____
S _____

Group

S _____
M _____
I _____
L _____
E _____
S _____

Group

S _____
M _____
I _____
L _____
E _____
S _____

Group

S _____
M _____
I _____
L _____
E _____
S _____

GENERALIZE

Forming a rule that explains a number of given situations.

Chapter 17. *John* could only read words written upside down.
Chapter 18. *Leslie* decides to sell her toes.

ACTIVITY

Step One Collect, organize, and examine the material. Briefly list what you know about these Wayside School students:

A. Joe   B. Sharie   C. Todd   D. Bebe   E: Calvin

F. Myron   G. Maurecia   H. Paul   I. Dana   J. Jason

K. Rondi   L. Sammy   M. Deedee   N. D.J.

Step Two Identify what these students have in common.

_____

_____

Step Three Make a generalization about Wayside students based on their common characteristics.

_____

_____

Step Four Find other examples from Wayside School that fit this generalization.

1. John _____
2. Leslie _____

Do John and Leslie have the same common characteristics as the other Wayside School students? _____

If so, the generalization you stated in Step Three is a good one.

Chapter 19. *Miss Zarves* - There is no Miss Zarves.

Chapter 20. *Kathy* thinks she has good reasons for hating everybody.

Chapter 21. *Ron* wants to play kickball but is poor at the game.

Write a List Chant about Wayside School students. Follow the Girl's Chant Pattern to write a Boy's Chant.

The Girl's Chant	The Boy's Chant

Girls of Wayside School
 	
    Sharie
    Sleeps a lot
    Babe
    Draws fast
    Maurecia
    Eats ice cream
These are just a few
    Dana
    Itches
    Rondi
    No teeth
    Deedee
    Always late
    Leslie's pigtails, too.
From near and far
Here they are
Girls of Wayside School
	Boys of Wayside School

PLAN

1. Determine what is to be done.
2. Determine needed materials.
3. List steps in order.
4. Predict problems.
5. Determine possibility of success.

Chapter 22. The three Erics
    Nice *Eric Oven* is called Crabapple.
    Good athlete *Eric Fry* is called Butterfingers.
    Skinny *Eric Bacon* is called Fatso just because they all have the same first name.
Chapter 23. *Allison* threatens to knock everybody's teeth out.

ACTIVITY

Make a plan so that the children will be able to tell the three Eric's apart and recognize the unique qualities of each.

EXAMPLE	YOUR PLAN

1. What I will do:
    Hang signs around their necks with the words:
        Athlete
        Skinny
        Nice
	1. What will I do:

2. Materials needed: poster board, markers, hole punch, string	2. Materials needed:
3. Steps: get materials, make signs, hang around necks, point to signs so others will notice them	3. Steps:

4. Possible problems:
    finding materials
    getting others to notice signs
	4. Possible problems:

5. Possibility of success: 50%	5. Possibility of success:

SEQUENCE

To order events or items according to ascending or descending size or value.

Chapter 24. *Dameon* can't figure out how to write his name on his pencil.

Chapter 25. *Jenny* is late to school and finds no one there.

ACTIVITY

Cut apart the strips to tell Dameon's and Jenny's stories. Add capital letters and punctuation marks where needed.

JENNY'S STORY	DAMEON'S STORY
1. she did her spelling and	1. and he
2. came in so did a bald	2. louis wanted to watch
3. a man with a mustache	3. and down the stairs
4. on a motorcycle	4. made three trips up
5. man jenny discovered	5. the movie Dameon
6. no one was there	6. the teacher told Dameon
7. jenny rode to school	7. missed the movie
8. it was Saturday	8. to run downstairs and see if

Correct order: 7, 4, 6, 1, 3, 2, 5, 8   *Correct order: 6, 8, 2, 5, 4, 3, 1, 7*

Chapter 26. *Terrence* is a poor sport and kicks balls over the fence until he gets kicked over the fence.

Chapter 27. *Joy* forgets her lunch and eats Dameon's, then accuses everyone else.

ACTIVITY

Complete the cause and effect statements about Terrence and Joy.

CAUSES	EFFECTS
	The children didn't want Terrence to play.
Terrence kicked the ball over the fence.	
	There were no more balls.
Louis picked Terrence up.	
	Joy was hungry.
	She could not eat in the lunchroom.
Dameon brought his lunch.	
Joy put wax paper on Allison's desk.	
	Joy wasn't hungry.

 © Nancy Polette

Chapter 28. *Nancy* is a boy who gets a new name.

Chapter 29. *Stephen* gets rid of the ghost of Mrs. Gorf.

Chapter 30. *Louis's* job was to make sure no one had too much fun at recess.

Below find a web of a typical school day.

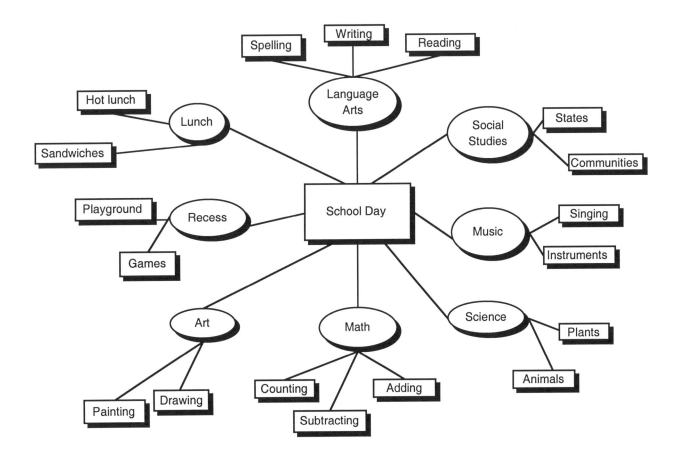

ACTIVITY

Make a web that shows a typical school day at Wayside School.

© Nancy Polette